D0979148

Men on the Moving Frontier

Men on the Moving Frontier

By Roger G. Kennedy

AMERICAN WEST PUBLISHING COMPANY

PALO ALTO / CALIFORNIA

Library of Congress Catalog Card Number 78-88203

This book is for Frances

"These men of the frontier were acutely self-conscious. By the time Minnesota, Wisconsin, and the Dakotas were settled it was no longer possible for an educated man to escape an awareness of how he should think of himself on the frontier, what his proper stance upon it should be. A literature of the West had grown up, and the ideals it set forth were a part of the intellectual inventory of all the men we will be watching through these pages, as they each in his own degree, were watching themselves. It is possible, therefore, to find in their stories not only a sequence of events but also a pattern of action; there was real history and also an imaginary, or hoped-for history. For some of them there was, in the imagination, only a grey world of duty or a silver world of profit. For others, this West offered an occasion for the assertion of heroic character, brightly colored and proud."

Contents

Chapter One

Character and Circumstance

I

THIS IS A TIME FOR TALISMANS. Black Americans wear upon their breasts, where bishops carry pectoral crosses, amulets made by African craftsmen in earnest of their heritage. I have seen black hands go up to touch those amulets in times of tension, as old Antaeus touched the earth.

In our house we have a talisman of bronze. It does not evoke the same intensity of feeling as a black amulet, for the tradition of which it speaks has not been repressed but merely undervalued. But it does serve to remind us of a past which contributes vitality to the present. Our talisman is cast from a design made in 1908 by Louis Sullivan and George Elmslie for a teller's wicket for a bank in a small city in southern Minnesota. It was not intended to be a museum piece, enshrined as "fine art." It was meant to be used in commerce. A bank teller peered through its bronze foliage and made change through the ornamented aperture at the base.

The building for which that wicket was designed, in Owatonna, stands amid the jumble of Main Street as if a colossal figure of Louis Sullivan were there, its arms spread out, its palms upward in invitation and exhortation. It is impossible to describe the effect upon a responsive observer of that warm reddish brick building, of its green and blue and gold terra-cotta, of the shimmer of its stained glass, just as it is impossible to put into words the effect of San Marco in the rain or the first sight of Rheims Cathedral. The Owatonna bank is a modern wonder, a triumph of character over circumstance.

That is what this book is about. There have been a hundred volumes written on the influence of the frontier on various presumed aspects of our national character. Sullivan and Elmslie's building is an expression, instead, of the influence of character upon the frontier. As the region between the Missouri River and the Great Lakes filled with settlers and then was organized into farms, towns, corporations, political parties, churches, and professions, it provided an opportunity for the display of character. At the outset, the frontier afforded an open scene, permitting almost total freedom, encouraging eccentricity. As the open spaces became overgrown with a thicket of organization, there were different, and probably diminishing, opportunities for self-expression.

To observe the effect of personality upon each phase of the socialization of this area, I have chosen pairs of characters, each set placed in a period in the frontier's history. First, two explorers, then two of the earliest political organizers, then two architects of the shape of the new cities, then two politicians of a rapidly solidifying social structure, and, finally, two artists who reflected the passing of the frontier.

Superficially, at least, the primary contrast between the two men paired in each period is that between a romantic temperament and one disposed toward successful and relatively unimaginative accommodation. But character cannot be confined in any capsule, realistic or romantic; from the contrast of real persons subordinate themes emerge. One is the effect of the heroic models chosen by each of these characters in shaping their own actions.* Another is the matter of success, the relationship between aspiration and realization. Third, one can observe the difference between the conventional assessments made upon

*If this were a work of social science this might be called something like "paradigmatic preconditioning."

these men by contemporary opinion and the reassessments of our own time.

Of much more importance than an attempt to make a case here for what should be pursuasively presented later is an effort at a definition of what is meant by romanticism. Modern spokesmen of the midwestern romantic tradition have used a curious vernacular, which does require some translation. William Gray Purcell, the last of the characters to be presented in these pages, lived until 1965, though his pattern of speech and belief was formed before the Civil War (for reasons which will appear in the chapter devoted to his long and useful life). Purcell was an advocate of the romantic strain in western life, and it is easiest to view that tradition as he did, rejoicing in the accomplishments of our own day and still insisting that we can do very much better to create a humane, expansive, and lively culture.

Purcell often said that "there is so much subjective romanticism in the average human that it should be the purpose of all of us to make it more objective, more tangible, more useful to him." What did he mean by "subjective romanticism"? He meant a desire to be free and generous, to be hopeful and bold. He meant to be frankly emotional, to be easily moved by friendship or beauty, and to hate humbug, pedantry, smugness, coldness of heart. Read in the air-conditioned, aseptic environment of the contemporary city—where some men think themselves uninhibited because they can talk to their analysts and read scrofulous novels—a call for romantic freedom may seem a little old fashioned. It is certainly not "news," nor was it, in 1900, new. Purcell and his fellow progressive architects were very conscious of standing in a long American tradition. Frank Lloyd Wright loved to quote this passage from Walt Whitman: "Going where I list, my own master... divesting myself of the holds that would hold me. I inhale great drafts of space. The east and the west are mine, and the north and the south are mine.... Beware what precedes the decay of the ruggedness of states and men. Beware of civilization."

That is the romantic accent heard throughout this book. A wariness of too much civilization led Giacomo Constantino Beltrami to seek out the savage West, and after him Henry Hastings Sibley sought a refuge from the steel hand of puritanism.

Ignatius Donnelly, once he had broken free of Alexander Ramsey's political machine, was never willing to surrender again; and Purcell, echoing Whitman, set forth the manifesto of progresivism in these words: "We desire the right to do for ourselves, feel for ourselves, love for ourselves, sustain the burden of the heritage of glory from the past for ourselves."

A second major theme of midwestern romanticism, which united such diverse characters as Beltrami, Harvey Ellis, Sibley, and Purcell, was a reverence for the Middle Ages. This was not mere antique collecting but an effort to recover a vitality which had suffered from the constrictions of classicism. Lewis Mumford, writing about William Morris, has pointed out recently that the Gothic revival of the eighteenth century "could with propriety be called the medieval Renaissance" and that it

> was an attempt to recover vital components of folk culture that purely upper-class groups, princes and artists, inventors and industrialists, had left out of their system. The medievalists were against classic book learning, esthetic formalism, and sophistication. Organic complexity, freedom of adaptation, respect for materials and processes, simplicity and sincerity—these were the new notes.

This is a precise description of the ideals which George Grant Elmslie, Purcell's partner, brought to America from Morrisite groups in Scotland. In Chicago he found an equally passionate commitment to this point of view, proceeding from the American Gothic revival and from a strong strain of romanticism persisting in the West. Beltrami, Sibley, Donnelly, Ellis, and Purcell all read the medieval chronicles, and all found inspiration in the Victorian writers who were calling for a rejection of the chilly intellectuality of classic culture. Such disparate concerns as courtly love, a humane Indian policy, the medieval (Romanesque) revival, the arts and crafts movement, and a belief in folk culture, all were nourished by the same revived medievalism. A sense of popular participation in the arts was as important to Ignatius Donnelly as it was to Purcell, who spoke of the cathedral builders as Morris might: "Once the art of architecture was so alive that all the people had a cordial and daily interest in the work of the builders. They were making fresh, simple, joyous things every day, and the people rejoiced because they were given what they could feel and given it in such a way that they felt . . . part of it."

There is an association between the arts and crafts movement and the frontier which has been largely overlooked. We have heard a great deal about the wastefulness of the pioneer, his despoiling the natural beauty of the West, his heedlessness of posterity in his rush for riches. This is one aspect of the frontier experience, but there is another. The frontier was a place where new tools were created, and new amenities for life. And this creation, arising out of necessity, was often done with care. Primitive conditions could produce beauty, and handwork could produce a respect for craftsmanship. Purcell, speaking of his journalist grandfather, said:

> From his pioneer boyhood days, all his life he had done homely chores, made useful things, taken good care of everything that had cost some man's time and labor. And in calling upon others to go and do likewise, to try to understand their world not only with their brains but with their hands, Grandfather . . . put the printed page to its best possible use.

Purcell recalled a neighbor in the woods of northwestern Wisconsin, "Uncle Billy" Green,

> a maker of things that would work, a fixer of things that would not work. The workbench, the self-closing gate in the garden fence, and the orderly stacked kindling wood, all spoke as dignified and self-sufficient units in a universal architecture, not because they were well-proportioned or patterned, but because through sweet and living material they had risen at the joyful call of jackknife and axe and understanding heart. He called them forth to be what they inevitably had to be. He whittled out a supply of tool handles. He set up on its post the big goblet of iron bars which, filled with pine knots, served as a torch. He made birch-pole ladders to reach the sleeping lofts, built cupboards, tables, and chairs, all of them simple, some of them crude and colored with human use.

The land where the rivers rise, as seen in Joseph Nicollet's famous 1842 map of the Upper Mississippi. In a little over a generation, this wilderness would be civilized—more or less—by a land-hungry army of farmers.

REGION OF ROCKS AND WATER
HUNTERS ISLAND
HEIGHTS
KICHI GUMMI
LAKE SUPERIOR
ILE ROYALE
CHIPEWAY COUNTRY
WISCONSIN
TERRITORY
WISCONSIN RIVER
WINEBAGO INDIAN COUNTRY
COUNTRY
WARPEKUTEY
Fort William
Ottawa L.
Court Oreilles L.
Shell L.
Mille Lacs
La Biche R.
Buffalo L.
Helena
Centreville
Prairie La Crosse
Battle of Bad Axe
Bad Axe R.
Upper Iowa R.
Turkey R.
Volga R.
L. Albert Lea
Rapids and Portage
Big Bull Falls
Little Bull Falls
Painted Rock
Pt. Atkinson
...SSISSIPPI_1842.
Julius Bien & Co. lith.

On the frontier, arts and crafts were not the outgrowth of an anti-industrial reaction; they were the products of need. In the West the arts and Crafts movement of the Old World gained a new vigor because many pioneers joined respect for craftsmanship with respect for innovation. Many devices familiar to the race as a whole had to be rediscovered by each pioneer for himself. He often went west with few tools and without the availability of the specialized skills for which he had looked to his neighbors. He had to make for himself new tools and develop his own competence to use them. Within a few years a pioneer community could become intensely specialized, but it took time for the tools to be made and the skills to grow. Each pioneer, except those few who went in colonies, had to recapitulate in a lifetime the long learning process of western civilization, drawing upon pattern books, memory, and an occasional passing tinker to help speed the process.

Innovation became one of the characteristics of western politics and western architecture. Men like Robert La Follette and Louis Sullivan, Ignatius Donnelly, and William Gray Purcell approached a problem as would a pioneer, seeking solutions without too much deference to authority or habit. It was inevitable, perhaps, that as the common experience of pioneering receded into memory, so would the habit of freedom from habit, the tradition of independence from tradition. Timorous souls could not keep up the pace, and there were many backsliders. But some never weakened. They were innovators, all their long lives, pioneers standing each morning on a new private frontier. They refused to be drugged by habit, intimidated by authority, or tyrannized by precedent.

This romantic individualism carries with it Whitman's resistance to the pulverizing of idiosyncrasy by society. The romantics sought privacy, freedom from distraction and intrusion, just as many of the pioneers did. Daniel Boone, tracked to his lair on the Missouri River in 1819 by the Long expedition, spoke of his desire to move on again, though old and crippled and weary. The neighborhood had become noisy with other woodchoppers. The barking of dogs had driven away the deer. A ring of nervousness was closing in. Boone wanted plenty of space at his elbows.

But that space need not necessarily be expressed in leagues or in sections of a new land. Thoreau found his quiet place within a mile or so of Concord, in an area settled for two centuries. There he did "live life with a wide margin," and out of a respect for nature and for things in daily use he developed a message which made romanticism relevant to the most city-pent of men.

The romantic tradition, very strong in Thoreau, makes intelligible Louis Sullivan's usually misappropriated dictum, "form follows function." Function has a special meaning in the romantic tradition. Absorbing earlier pantheistic romantic ideas in the early nineteenth century, Samuel Taylor Coleridge developed his concept that everything had a spirit, a soul, which determines its character. It is the business of the artist to discover what the proper form of the thing is, according to that spirit. Horatio Greenough, a little later than Coleridge, said that this "organic" molding of forms to spirit was the mission of furniture makers and of city planners, relevant "from a bedstead to a cathedral."

Purcell would insist that "the outward Form of the needed parts must . . . be useful in more ways than as mere elements of support and structure. They must state the quality of the entire enterprise. . . . The architect of a successful building is really not a designer, an originator—but an organizer, a discoverer, one who tries to find something that already exists."

And so we come to that teller's wicket in our front hall, a symbol of a romantic commitment to the relevance of beauty to the daily lives of people. Purcell, Sullivan, and Elmslie worked in the full assurance of a century's commitment to put art in the service of the people—even the people working in a bank!

> How . . . can we surmise that an American bank has no soul of its own seeking expression, or by what mental process are we going to ignore the deep fundamental principle underlying true art and say our building has no soul, and to believe that whether we clothe it as a Greek temple or a Roman temple makes no difference. Well, poor little bank! We believe we represent a philosophy that is wide enough to include a bank with a human being, with a picture, with a statue, with a steel bridge, with an automobile, or any fittingly executed work of the artist or artisan.

Insistent creativity, reverence for beauty as a part of daily living, places art in the marketplace. The romantic progressives were concerned with "not what a building will appear like [in a presentation drawing] but what it is going to be, out in the rain and sun, among people, attending to its business effectively and being interesting to everyone every business hour of the day." The strenuous individuality of the creator, channeled through a reverence for the common materials of the region and the common uses of things, has in it sufficient vitality and dedication to create a great civilization. This is the significance of the midwestern romantic tradition.

Finally, before presenting the drama of the shameless self-dramatist Giacomo Beltrami, it might be well to emphasize again how the western romantic tradition differed from that of the eastern seaboard, where a long line of genteel writers, colonialist in inclination, looked to Europe for models and often for material. There a complaint was voiced in almost identical terms by Hawthorne, Bryant, Cooper, and William James that America could not produce romantic literature because it was "a country where there is no shadow, no antiquity, no mystery, no picturesque and gloomy wrong, no anything but a commonplace prosperity, in broad and simple daylight. . . . Romance and poetry, ivy, lichens and wall-flowers need ruin to make them grow."

So fixed were these American writers upon European models that they missed the fire of the frontier drama. They wrote of the West as journalists or tourists, patronizing it lest they be patronized by their European paradigms; or they wrote as Cooper did, seeking to dress in a false medievalism characters who were amply romantic on their own merit. The best architects of the Greek revival tried to originate, not imitate; to "think like Greeks," not to "build like Greeks." In the same spirit, American writers might have sought to think like the craftsmen of the Middle Ages, respecting the materials before them, rather than seeking to imitate Sir Walter Scott.

It is ironic that Europeans like Beltrami came to the frontier because they thought of it as romantic while American writers like Hawthorne turned their backs upon it and sought to find romance in Italy. Early nineteenth-century American writers along the Atlantic littoral kept American romantic literature colonial. A generation later Daniel Burnham and his colleagues almost succeeded in subjugating midwestern romantic architecture and making it colonial. That is another part of the story to be told in this book.

It is another irony that the men of the American frontier were themselves quite capable of investing their lives with the romanticism which the colonial writers could not see. To Henry Hastings Sibley the American West was a grand arena for the romantic drama. It is the failure of American writers from Hawthorne to Fitzgerald to see it so, to acknowledge the presence of that drama on their doorstep, that made them, even at their best, so artificial.

This is not, however, a work of literary criticism, nor does it attempt intellectual history in the grand Parringtonian style. It is a gallery of portraits with commentary, rather like those walls of museums where extinct pioneers peer out upon us, escaping anonymity only by the feeble grace of a few typewritten lines set in tarnished card-holders. Here we have a little more space than those identifying resumés to set them against the terrain in which they once moved.

II

THESE STORIES ARE SET in the land where the rivers rise. Northward, the long swamps ooze toward Hudson Bay; eastward the St. Lawrence begins its erratic passage, trickling through the rocks and muskeg toward the series of deep basins —Superior, Huron, Michigan, Ontario, and Erie; and, finally, surging over rapids, tearing at the sides of rocky islands, it pours out into the Atlantic. Southward, a thousand streams wander down the tilted prairie, finding allies joining new groups under limestone bluffs, broadening and strengthening, until all are gathered into the onrush of the Mississippi-Missouri system.

The first Europeans who groped up these streams into the central valley may have come from the north or the east. Certainly the French were on Lake Superior by 1620, and they knew the interior of Wisconsin well before the men of Massachusetts Bay were very certain of the contours of the Berkshires. In thinking about the politics of the seventeenth and eighteenth centuries in North America, one should recall that the Mississippi and St. Lawrence rivers provided two invasion routes into the heart of the continent which met at right angles in Minnesota, with a few stream-and-portage shortcuts through Wisconsin blunting the angle.

It is also useful to observe the alternation of emphasis between these systems until the last part of the nineteenth century. The east-west, horizontal route was most important while the fur trade drew pelts out of the vast lake region into the markets of Montreal. Then, when Indian and colonial wars obstructed it and the prime pelts came from the upper Missouri, steamboats made the Mississippi the spine of the West. New England politicians had good cause for anxiety: westerners looked to St. Louis and New Orleans, not to New York or Boston, for a market and culture. When the railroads reached the Mississippi in the 1850s and drew off its traffic, the needle of the compass turned again, pointing eastward through Chicago to New York. The Erie Canal had made it possible for New York to compete with New Orleans for western goods, but the railroads completed the link and united the North.

Railroads and highways have occupied our minds for fifty years. We pass high over the rivers on steel trestles or roil the surfaces of suburban streams, but we have forgotten what it was like to head upstream against a river in its spring rush. Francis Parkman, with his gift for imagining himself back into the heroic world in which man directly faced midwestern nature, saw the rivers as the early explorers saw them.

> The Missouri ... fierce, reckless, headstrong, exulting in its tumultuous force, it plays a thousand freaks of wanton power; bearing away forests from its shores, and planting them, with roots uppermost, in its quicksands; sweeping off islands, and rebuilding them; frothing and raging in foam and whirlpool, and, again, gliding, with dwindled current along its sandy channel. At length, dark with uncurbed fury, it pours its muddy tide into the reluctant Mississippi. ...

Homesteaders crossed the Mississippi carrying in their wagons everything they could for a new life in a hard land. Some managed to bring the family piano, which was a reminder of home as well as a guarantee of respectability.

> the disturbing power prevails ... and the united torrent bears onward in its might, boiling up from the bottom, whirling in many a vortex, flooding its shores with a malign deluge fraught with pestilence and fever, and burying forests in its depths, to ensnare the heedless voyager.

The source of the Mississippi lies within what has always been a frontier—a borderland. Before men came into the region, two frontiers intersected there, as they still intersect today. One straggles vaguely north and south, green against brown as the pinelands strike the prairie. The empire of the pine was the St. Lawrence watershed, extending into central Minnesota and an area covering the northern curlings of the Mississippi. Between it and the open grassland there was an intermediate zone of hardwood clumps, which ended on the shore of the vast dry lake-bed which has become the Red River Valley, where the wind has to contend with only a few bedraggled cottonwoods.

East and west lies another ancient transition zone, between the deep brown soil of the central valley and the rock, swamp, and muskeg of the arctic littoral. In northern Minnesota, farms and pastures abandon their effort, leaving the scene to wolves, moose, and migrating birds. It was not until the middle of the nineteenth century that the agricultural frontier was recognized to lie so far north as that. Prairie du Chien, in southwestern Wisconsin, was believed to be the farthest possible outpost of farmers. The assumption that the domain of the arctic extended into central Minnesota and Wisconsin was one of the chief attractions of the region for some men, as we shall see. Though the country was gentle in contour and well provided with water, it was also cold, remote, and exposed to a vicious wind, and few were willing to predict that it would be hospitable to masses of settlers.

At the beginning of the sixteenth century, streams of explorers, exploiters, and settlers went out of Europe into the Americas, Africa, and Australia. There they created new Europes in which the aborigines were either assimilated, penned into reservations, or eradicated. Across the middle of North America, after it had been crossed by exploration from the east and the south, there came a rush of land-hungry farmers. They devoured the area in chunks. The census statistics show a surprisingly orderly pattern of occupation, state by state, decade by decade. The great surges came in sequence:

	1800	*1810*	*1820*	*1830*	*1840*	*1850*	*1860*
Ohio	45,000	231,000					
Indiana		24,000	147,000				
Illinois			55,000	157,000			
Wisconsin					31,000	305,000	
Minnesota						6,000	169,000

Then, of course, the frontier moved on. It passed over the prairie like a summer storm, a stage curtain drawn across the land. In the two decades between 1870 and 1890, the population of the Dakotas grew from 14,000 to 510,000 while Indiana, Illinois, and Wisconsin were already sending on more people than they were gaining by in-migration. Finally, the squall line swirled and separated; the census of 1890 stated that "the unsettled area has been so broken into by isolated bodies of settlement that there can hardly be said to be a frontier."

As the frontier passed over the land where the rivers rise, it passed through the lives of the men whose stories are told in this book. It provided the circumstance upon which the character of each worked. F. Scott Fitzgerald and William Gray Purcell were born in the Middle West, but each of the others had come into the region for a reason. Giacomo Constantino Beltrami was in search of a backdrop for a performance, a scene for adventure. Stephen Harriman Long, the dour and meticulous engineer, decomposed Beltrami's stage setting into its contour lines and its azimuths.

Henry Hastings Sibley sought to go beyond the frontier to find freedom, and did not go far enough—he was engulfed by civilization. His friend Alexander Ramsey, the proconsul, went out to the frontier to profit by the changes it would cause and grew rich. Ignatius Donnelly began as one of Ramsey's minions and ended as the cranky, courageous voice of those who felt they had been cheated of the frontier's promise. Frank Billings Kellogg, who had once been a constituent of Donnelly's, speedily put behind him his kinship with the struggling farmers and carried into high office the smugness of those the frontier had favored with its bounty. That bounty provided for an artistic flowering, and two who benefited from, and contributed to, that flowering were Harvey Ellis, the vagrant genius of architecture, and Daniel Burnham, the tycoon of the profession.

F. Scott Fitzgerald was born into the generation which inherited the fruits of the frontier (in great or small profusion according to the good fortune of their fathers). He developed his characteristic snobbery in a city which was settling down, becoming respectable, developing an inherited social structure. His graceful style and social sensitivity made him a superb expositor of the events of the "second act" in American lives, which began after the frontier had passed.

William Gray Purcell was half a generation older than Fitzgerald, and he survived the poet of the Jazz Age by twenty-four years. Intellectually, however, he was a contemporary of Thoreau and Emerson. He was, therefore, peculiarly fitted to survey the whole scene, from the years when the frontier first reached Minnesota to the present.

These men of the frontier were acutely self-conscious. By the time Minnesota, Wisconsin, and the Dakotas were settled, it was no longer possible for an educated man to escape an awareness of how he should think of himself on the frontier, what his proper stance upon it should be. A literature of the West had grown up, and the ideals it set forth were a part of the intellectual inventory of all the men we will be watching through these pages, as they, each in his own degree, were watching themselves. It is possible, therefore, to find in their stories not only a sequence of events but also a pattern of action: there was a real history and also an imaginary or hoped-for history. For some of them there was, in the imagination, only a gray world of duty or a silver world of profit. For others, the Midwest offered an occasion for the assertion of heroic character, brightly colored and proud.

Chapter Two

Giacomo Constantino Beltrami

Stephen Harriman Long

I

ROMANCE AND SCIENCE were uneasy partners in the exploration of the American West. The engineers who mapped the geology of the region, listed its landmarks, skinned and classified its birds and mammals, and carried homeward in their saddlebags the dried husks of its insects were not disinterested scientists. They were engaged in a great enterprise in occupation, preempting the interior of the continent from the ambitions of the French, the Spanish, or the Russians, and for eighty years continuously seeking to deny the Mississippi Valley to that British power which brooded on the north and west. Lewis and Clark, Zebulon Pike, and Stephen Long were the most celebrated of these systematic instruments of policy.

There were also the romantic explorers, who had no interest whatever in continental power relationships and sought, in the West, a series of scenes upon which to display themselves. It was a concession by history to comedy that the quintessential engineer, dour, surly, methodical Stephen Long, was accompanied on one of his most important explorations by the fantastic Giacomo Beltrami, playwright, producer, and protagonist of a pageant which took seventy-six years to perform.

Their meeting was a consequence of the geopolitics of John C. Calhoun. In the years after the War of 1812, President Monroe's ambitious secretary of war developed a grand design for calming the Indian tribes, protecting the fur trade, and obstructing British influence in the extremities of the Louisiana Purchase. The Lewis and Clark expedition had secured information about a narrow pathway to the Pacific, but all about it there remained a vastness of rumor and potential peril. Calhoun determined to send exploration parties to extend American knowledge and plan American occupation of the upper reaches of the Missouri-Mississippi system. His primary agent for these endeavors was Major Stephen Harriman Long of the U.S. Army's Corps of Engineers.

Long had been born in the Puritan village of Hopkinton, New Hampshire, in 1784 and had graduated from Dartmouth College in 1809. After teaching for a few years, he entered the army during the War of 1812 but, displaying his lifelong penchant for avoiding glory, was assigned to administrative chores. In 1816 he became a teacher of mathematics at West Point and in the next year began a reconnaissance of the West which led him, according to his own account, to explore far more territory than had Lewis and Clark but with far less fame. He first traveled the southwestern area between the Arkansas and Red rivers, then, in 1817, the valley of the Upper Mississippi as far as the present sites of St. Paul and Minneapolis.

In 1818 Calhoun instructed Long to form an expedition to investigate the headwaters of the Missouri's central tributaries, the Arkansas and the Platte. This expedition did its field work in the period 1819–20 and set out again two years later with a refreshed staff to assert the American presence in the region to the west and north of Fort Snelling in Minnesota. It was on that tour that Long was accompanied by Beltrami—with dire consequences.

After his return from Minnesota and the publication of his report on his travels, Long undertook surveys for the Baltimore and Ohio Railway. In 1829 he published the first American treatise on railroad engineering and in 1836 a pioneering text on bridge building. In 1861, as the Civil War broke out and younger colleagues set out on heroic exploits, Long, at the age of 76, finally became chief of the Corps of Topographical Engineers and spent the early years of the great conflict sending maps to field commanders. He was finally mustered out in 1863 and died the following year in Alton, Illinois.

It is difficult to find in all of Long's letters, reports, and the books written by his companions a single instance in which this brave, honorable, and hopelessly drab character expressed rapture or even exhilaration. He was, consistently, unimpressed by the continent he explored and gloomy about its prospects. As a young man he toured the richest farming region of the eastern seaboard, around Lancaster County, Pennsylvania, and found it depressing; its villages, Lancaster, York, Reading, and Norristown were, he said, "sinks of dissipation and debauchery." When later he reached the site of Chicago, he pronounced it unfit for either commerce or agriculture. Long and his chronicler, Major Edwin James, have a sort of notoriety in some history books for sharing the responsibility for providing the American public with the concept that the Great Plains were a great American desert. They called the region "almost wholly unfit for cultivation, and of course uninhabitable by a people depending upon agriculture for their subsistence."

In his way, a somber way indeed, Long had encouraging words for the region now occupied by Denver, Colorado Springs, and Boulder: it could "serve as a barrier to prevent too great an extension of our population westward." Major James went on to say that as a barrier zone it was "an unfit residence for any but a nomad population.... The traveler who shall at any time have traversed its desolate sands will, we think, join us in the wish that this region may for ever remain the unmolested haunt of the native hunter, the bison, and the jackal."

It has been said in defense of Long that he was not congenitally cheerless but was, instead, a precise observer who simply lacked the imagination to conceive of what irrigation and the railroad could do in the absence of navigable streams and supplies of native wood. But water and wood aplenty were to be

Giacomo Constantino Beltrami, the "poet in a pack of engineers," as rendered in his superbly romanticized A Pilgrimage in Europe and America Leading to the Discovery of the Sources of the Mississippi *(London, 1828).*

found in Minnesota. What was his impression of its lush green prairieland, interspersed with groves of hardwoods and bordered by a million acres of pine trees? West of Lake Superior, he said, was "a sterile dreary waste." According to the Long expedition, the valley of the Minnesota River (then thick with prairie grass, now lush with grain that supports a score of prosperous towns) was a desolation.

> [There are] no buffalo ranging across the prairies, no deer stalking through the forests, no birds interrupting the solemn stillness which uniformly reigns over the country.... Where game is scarce, the Indian of course finds no inducement to hunt, and hence the party frequently traveled for whole days without seeing a living object of any kind.

Giacomo Constantino Beltrami, on the other hand, was transported by the beauty of the same landscape. Indeed, his response to the region was so rapturous that a grateful state legislature (which named not so much as a roadside rest stop for Long) celebrated Beltrami with a county and with a park known as Count Beltrami State Monument. Beltrami would have been delighted. A lifelong aspiration was fulfilled: he was many things, but he was not a count. He was born in Bergamo, Italy, in 1779, the tenth child of a Venetian customs officer. Early in life he determined that a bureaucratic existence was not for him and that instead he would become "a hero of romance." Imbued with the ideals of the French Revolution, he put his education in the law at the service of Napoleon's dominance of Italy from 1807 to 1812, grudgingly acceded to the "restoration" after Waterloo, achieved a local magistracy, but became embroiled in a plot of the *carabinieri* and was exiled in 1821.

Two years later, after wandering in Europe and America, he found himself in Pittsburgh, at the forks of the Ohio River, with a vague dream of capping the achievements of his countrymen, Columbus, the Cabots, Vespucci, and Verrazano, by discovering the headwaters of the Mississippi.* Here the exiled hero en-

*This was a time in which intrepid Europeans were pursuing great rivers to their origins in several dark continents. While Beltrami was at the forks of the Ohio, contemplating an ascent of the Mississippi, Oudney, Denham, and Clapperton were struggling toward Lake Chad, and the Niger, Congo, and Amazon were also being explored.

countered just the man he needed, the agent of the UnitedStates government commissioned to tend the Indian tribes of the upper Mississippi, Major Lawrence Taliaferro. The major was impressed by Beltrami: "six feet high, of commanding appearance and some forty-five years of age; proud of bearing and quick of temper, high spirited, but always a gentleman. He expressed an earnest wish to explore the sources of the Mississippi. I gave him a passport to go where he pleased."

Together they traveled as far as Taliaferro's post at Fort Snelling, where the Mississippi is joined by the Minnesota River. Shortly after Beltrami reached the fort with Taliaferro, Long's party arrived. From this point, the tale must be told largely in Beltrami's words, for Long, in his official account, constrained his side of the story to a footnote: "An Italian whom we met at Fort St. Anthony [Snelling] attached himself to the expedition and accompanied us to Pembina. He has recently published a book . . . which we notice merely on account of the fictions and misrepresentations which it contains. S.H.L."

While Beltrami was with them, they had no choice but to notice him, for he was a poet in a pack of engineers, and his was the poetry of action. Beltrami would wander off from a night's encampment to be transported with delight at a moon-drenched glade. When they were intent upon maintaining scientific detachment, he sought to feel and record "every impression which so novel a scene is capable of producing." To them the scene must be broken into its physical components; to him it was a stimulant for "feelings I cannot describe . . . feelings which perhaps no other scene could awaken." Often "in this remote and central wilderness, my heart and mind are filled with the most delightful emotions." One day, while recording the course of granite outcrops, they found him spread-eagled upon a boulder and moist with "tears of gratitude and attachment." He luxuriated in the exquisite "emotions which . . . agitate my heart."

Not unexpectedly, Long and his associates regarded Beltrami with annoyance. He, on the other hand, regarded them as clods. Minnesota, to him, was a theater for "feelings of intense and new delight. The sublime traits of nature; phenomena which fill the soul with astonishment, and inspire it at the same time with almost heavenly ecstasy! ... sentiments of faith and piety, perfect and profound. ..." To them Minnesota was merely terrain traversed by fauna, some of which ate each other. They did everything possible to induce him to experience his transports privately. Then they set about to make his life sufficiently grim to induce him to depart.

At the outset Long was barely courteous; he could tell in a few minutes that Taliaferro proposed to bed him with a dervish. He sought to discourage the Italian by tales of the terrors of the country, which, of course, merely ignited Beltrami's heroic instincts. "Major Long did not cut a very noble figure in the affair; I foresaw all the disgusts and vexations I should have to experience. Nonetheless, I was obliged to sacrifice my pride and my feeling of what was due to me ... and to give myself up to all I foresaw I should have to endure from littleness and jealousy."

They set out on July 7, 1823, turning away from the Mississippi itself and following instead the Minnesota River valley, which progresses southwesterly for a hundred miles or more before turning northwestward again to proceed in parallel to the Mississippi. Long's commission required him to follow the Minnesota to its source, then to continue northward along the Red River until he located the Canadian border, and then finally to turn eastward to explore that border. Beltrami was content to join the expedition because he thought the Red, Minnesota, and Mississippi rivers all had their origins in the same plateau.

On the second day out Long's men tried a new method to discourage their companion. Beltrami reported that, crossing the river in a small boat, "my sailors were so deficient either in strength or skill, that they suffered it to be carried away by the current and dashed in pieces against a rock, upon which I remained perched." He does not report either how he escaped his perch or what happened to the "sailors," but it is difficult to regard this as an accident, especially in view of his trials of the night of July 11:

> Our tent being open on both sides ... the major ... had the attention to place me on one of the two sides of the tent, in order, no doubt, that I might observe the weather at my

Major Stephen Harriman Long in 1823: he did not, in Beltrami's opinion, "cut a very noble figure," an important consideration to the romantic Italian.

> ease, and reap the glory of struggling valiantly against the fury of the wind, rain, hail, thunder, and lightning.

On July 13:

> We might have had some good shooting, and the *savans* among us might have gained new and valuable ornithological information, but the major was intent on *making an expedition* and consulted nothing but his compass: it was sufficient for him to say, "I have been there."

Beltrami would never have found it sufficient to say so little. At the mouth of the Brandy River he went to view the countryside and "went alone, that the delicious reverie it threw me into might not be broken by cold-heartedness or presumption." Later he had another romantic spell: "Tears filled my eyes. . . . I should have given myself up to its sweet influence had I not been with people who had no idea of stopping for anything but a broken saddle. . . ."

When Beltrami refused to be deterred by marooning, exposure, or studied cold-heartedness, Long resorted to mystification. He "carefully concealed . . . the exact geographical location" of the source of the Minnesota River when that point was reached, and, farther along, kept the findings of his instruments from Beltrami so that the latitude and longitude of Pembina, a settlement on the Red River, were husbanded "with more care than the priests of Thibet conceal their Grand Lama."

Beltrami responded by carefully amassing data to be used later in disparaging Long's professional reputation as an Indian negotiator. On July 17 "the major pronounced a speech, which appeared probably very good to his government, whose . . . generosity, he greatly extolled, but very bad to the Indians, since it concluded with the information that he had nothing to give them, and accordingly neither the chiefs nor anybody else made the slightest answer." Beltrami, to whom each newly encountered Indian tribe might be the elusive exemplars of Rousseau's noble savage, wanted the pleasure of joining them in their quaint native pastimes. "I begged the major to endeavor to induce the chief to give us the sight of a buffalo hunt with bows and arrows, but he replied, with his usual complaisance, that he could not stop." Long had information to gather and a report to deliver. Beltrami, in perpetual revolt against all forms of governmental authority and temperamentally averse to bureaucratic necessity, found the major's frequent writing of reports a constant irritation. To him the elaborate and painstaking process of scientific exploration was not only vexing to the free spirit but needless as well.

> A single individual, possessed of practical philosophy and genuine philanthropy, with a moderate knowledge of geography and astronomy, would . . . accomplish much more than an expedition fitted out at great expense. . . . The advantages which have been hitherto derived from these expeditions have not, I believe, answered the views of the government, or the expectations of the public. They have consisted of a few plants, with which perhaps all but the members of the expedition were acquainted, and which swell that mass of unintelligible hyeroglyphics, that scientific but tasteless and terrifying nomenclature, unfortunately consecrated by a great name, serving merely to overlay the memory and to blot out the lovely picture of nature; a few gaudy butterflies and other insects, of which we have already too many everywhere; of birds, which can only satisfy curiosity and luxury; of stones, suggesting a thousand conjectures of their nature and origin, and which . . . serve as materials for the idle discussions of pretenders to science, but contribute little or nothing to the benefit of the public; such have been the principal results of these pompous and costly enterprises.

Finally, at Pembina, the break came. Beltrami, for once, is silent about the proximate cause. Long's diary carries an entry under August 7, 1823: "Mr. Beltrami, our Italian companion, having taken offense at the party, generally, and being highly provoked at my objecting to his turning an Indian out of our lodge, left the party in a very hasty and angry manner."

Major Taliaferro gives a brief version of the next part of the story, emphasizing the loss of a horse which he had lent Beltrami. "At Pembina, a difficulty occurred between Major Long and Beltrami, when the latter sold his horse (my horse) and equipments [Long's account book indicates that the price was

$90.00], and in company with a half-breed passed near the line of 49 degrees to the sources of the Mississippi. His sufferings were of no agreeable nature."

Beltrami's sufferings began soon after he left Pembina and were increased by his refusal to demean himself by adapting too much to the requirements of survival in a bog. He made his way over the prairie to a small stream, which he followed happily by canoe until the Chippewa guides who were willing to paddle him upstream were terrified by a Sioux war party and deserted him. He had had ample opportunity to learn the simple technique of navigating a canoe with a paddle, but he scorned to learn such an exercise, apparently associated in his mind with lower-class folk like gondoliers. Thus, he proceeded up the wandering watercourse through an interminable swamp dragging the canoe by a rope. This is not, today, a pleasant countryside to traverse by automobile, less pleasant on foot even when protected by gnat and mosquito repellents. To wade through fifty miles of it towing a canoe, grubbing for food, drenched by rainstorms and unable to sleep because of the stinging of insects: that was a test for any "hero of romance."

Finally, the river became too deep to wade, and after an unsuccessful effort to learn "how to guide a canoe with an oar," Beltrami propped up his bright red umbrella in the bottom of the canoe to cover his equipage and continued on alone, wading, splashing, slipping, and floundering upstream. After four days of such trials, he had the good fortune to meet a client of Taliaferro's. The Indian agent later was at pains to explain why his influence twice made it possible for Beltrami, who by then had become internationally celebrated, to proceed with his adventures:

> He fell in with a sub-chief, the "Cloudy Weather," most fortunately, who know Mr. B., having seen him in one of my councils at the agency. The old man was given, by signs, to know that the white man wanted to descend the river. The chief took our Italian friend in his canoe, and turned down stream. Indians are proverbially slow, hunting and fishing on the way; Beltrami lost all patience, abused his Indian crew, made many menaces, etc. The "Cloud" tapped him on the hat with his pipe stem, as much as to say, "I will take

> you to my father safe, if you will be still." The old chief told of this temper of my friend, but Mr. B. never made allusion to it....

Taliaferro's friend "Mr. B," with Cloudy Weather's aid, almost discovered the source of the Mississippi. But source-finding is a tricky, scientific business, and Beltrami was in a hurry. He did discover a small lake lying between the watersheds of the Red River and the Mississippi. The lake was, appropriately for him, heartshaped, and in the middle of it water boiled up from an unfathomable depth. It had, he said, no visible issue. He pronounced it to be the source of both rivers, by filtration, and he named it Lake Julia, after a lady—"not my wife," he told Taliaferro, "but a lovely woman." Meddlesome surveyors have since found its outlet into the Red River chain through a neighboring pond named Puposky or Mud Lake.

But details were of little concern to Beltrami. For him the supreme moment was reached beside the little heartshaped lake, in the midst of a vast, oozing bog: "I feel with pride, that I have been more than human in not trembling then ... and the phenomenon of that lake, which is only surmounted by the Heavens! ... Those enchanting situations! That silence! That sombre solitude! My poor savage repast! My bark porringer! What an assemblage of wonders, of thoughts, and of feelings, surrounding the eyes, and the soul!"

Beltrami was always as conscious of the effect of his writing upon the reader as the effect of Lake Julia upon himself: "Let us only stop here a moment to allow some souls of sensibility to consecrate again their tears of regret and veneration to the most pure virtue...."

Virtue was important to Beltrami. He repeatedly reassured his readers of his own and extolled that of the women for whom he named North American landmarks. His relationship with women in general is too complex to record at this point, but it is worth noting that his adventures included surviving a drunken brawl among the Indians at Leach Lake through the timely intervention of a squaw. She appears only briefly as "the beautiful Woascita." When recounting this part of the tale, Beltrami asserted that "the picture of the dreadful Bacchanals

From Fort Snelling (seen above in 1851), Long's party set out for the wilderness that Beltrami craved. To the Italian's disgust, Long refused to take part in a buffalo hunt; such a scene (below) was painted in 1845 by John Stanley, whose savages appear nearly as noble as Beltrami might have wished.

at Leach Lake is of a sorrow entirely new, and I believe that the terrible dangers from which I have escaped ... may effect the reader of sensibility."

The effect upon Cloudy Weather and his Chippewas of encountering the waterlogged hero under his red umbrella must have been deeply satisfying to Beltrami's theatrical instincts. It must also have satisfied that sense of humor which flickers through his prose.

Beltrami thought he had achieved his end, the discovery of the Mississippi's source. He continued down the Mississippi, admonished by Cloudy Weather's pipe stem. At the end of September he arrived at Fort Snelling, to the amazement of the garrison, which had heard from the commandant's son that Beltrami had disappeared after leaving Pembina and was presumed to have died in the swamps.

After a few days at the fort, talking about his experiences (the commandant and his family "were indignant against Major Long for acting toward me in the miserable manner that he did"), Beltrami took a keelboat to St. Louis and New Orleans. There he published an account of his adventures in French. In the next few years he crossed Mexico from east to west, returned to the United States, and then briefly settled in London. He produced a two-volume, English-language version of his adventures in America, and two years later, in Paris, he brought out two more volumes on Mexico. After further wandering, he finally returned to Italy in his seventieth year and died at Filotrano in February 1855.

II

THE OUTLINE OF THE STORY is very simple: Major Stephen Harriman Long and "Count" Giacomo Constantino Beltrami spent an exasperating summer together in 1823, and each did his duty as he saw it. It is not difficult to ascertain from what Long said of himself and what others reported of him that his duty was very clear: to follow orders, to accept the policies established by other men, and to fulfill the description they provided of conduct proper to an officer. His interior plan, or, to put it in our contemporary jargon, his image of himself, did not transcend any directives he received from his superiors. Because we cannot detect any tension between his character and his circumstances, between his chores and his aspirations, he emerges as a stolid personality. Perhaps that is also why there remains as his cenotaph only the mountain peak he named for himself, and though it looms nearly as large and as high as Pike's, no one has ever sworn to make Long's peak or bust. No county, no state monument was ever set aside for him by the Minnesota legislature, though he explored more of the West than Lewis and Clark. Honors went instead to the Italian romantic who failed to discover the source of the Mississippi River.

Beltrami emerges from even the most derisive descriptions of his contemporaries as a man whose requirements for himself were so intense that he could almost force others to take him seriously. His insistence upon his heroic role was so vehement that he could not be set down as a mere posturer. To understand his power, it is necessary to probe somewhat more deeply into the components of his heroic insistence.

There was no doubt in Beltrami's mind about the man he meant to be. When he achieved the standard he had set, he said so with pride. "My constancy against difficulties perpetually increases.... The lists are always open; I feel as yet firm in the saddle, and shall sustain, be assured, many a shock and conflict before I surrender." When he finally found, in his solitary encampment at Lake Julia, a moment worthy of his dream, he imagined himself surrounded by a congratulatory assembly led by his historic countrymen, Columbus, the Cabots, Vespucci, and Verrazano. He had selected America for his arena, their America, and he felt them to be associates in his endeavor.

Why America? For an Italian, it was a strange and distant place, serviceable, therefore, for romantic exploits and attractive because national pride proclaimed it to be an Italian discovery, named by Italians. The requirements of romantic heroism always include distance from the audience—distance in time, distance in place, distance in culture. Beltrami's audience, like Byron's, was civilized Europe, and what Byron said of Albania, Beltrami

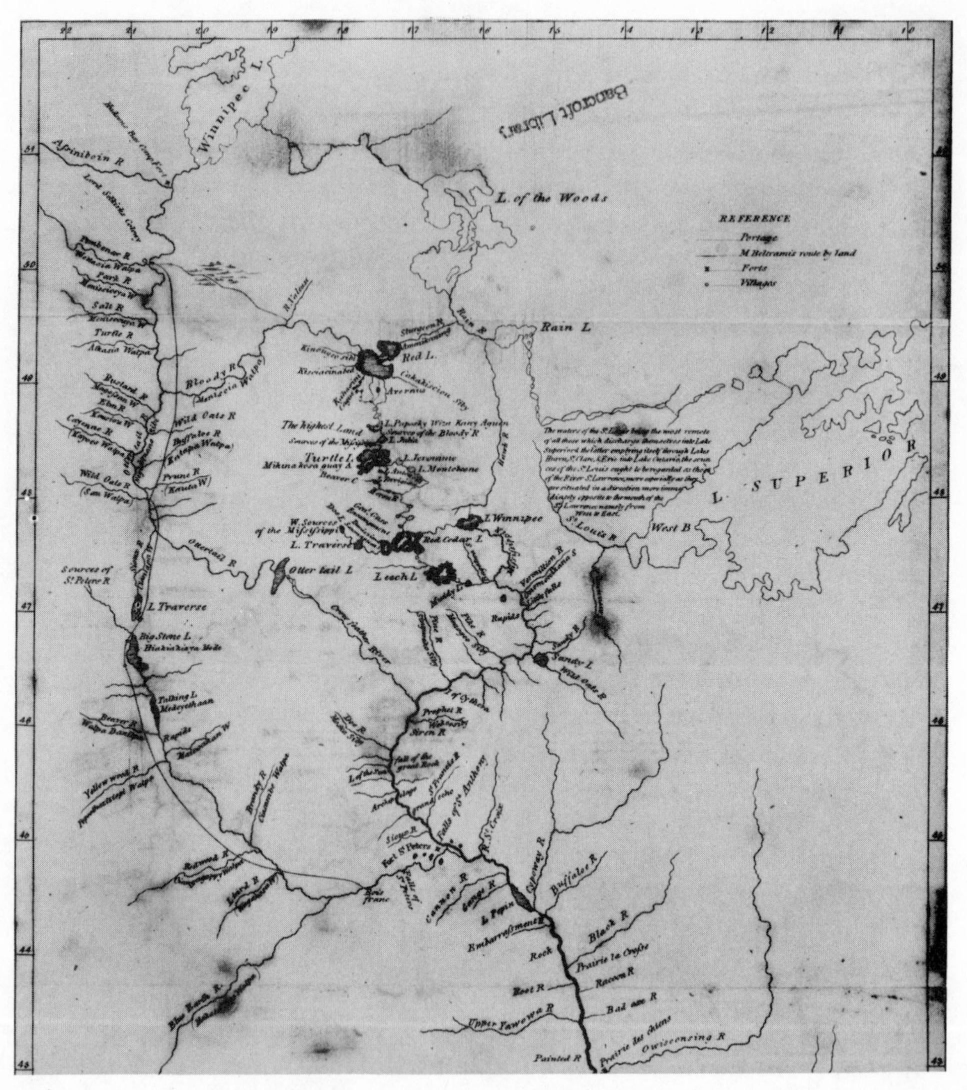

Beltrami's map of 1828, showing his version of the "Sources of the Mississippi"—the tiny, heart-shaped Lake Julia, a body of water between Turtle Lake and Red Lake in the top center of the map. He was wrong—but details were of little importance to Beltrami, who believed more in style than fact.

could have said of America: "The scene was savage—the scene was new." Distance and novelty were necessary: savagery was a pleasant accessory.* To an Italian who grew up amid moldering ruins and ancient, festering feuds, the heroic requirement of strangeness meant that he must seek a fresh and empty scene.

America was a popular candidate. Its novel republican experiment was very much in the minds of rebellious European intellectuals. Disappointed by the restoration of the "legitimacy," which placed again upon the thrones of Europe the inept lot Napoleon had sent waddling from their thrones to island refuges, they looked to America for a new chance, a new race of heroes. The frontiersmen, of whom Daniel Boone was the best known in Europe, seemed to be such a race. Major Edwin James, chronicler of the Long expedition, had reported after a visit to Boone in 1819 that the old man felt that it was time to move when he could no longer fell a tree for fuel so that its top would lie close to the door of his cabin: too broad a clearing meant too long a residence and too many neighbors. James's report was published and widely read in 1823. The next year Lord Byron wrote into the Eighth Canto of *Don Juan* a digression on Boone's condition:

> The lust which stings, the splendor which encumbers
> With the free forester divide no spoil
> Stern, not sullen, were the solitudes
> Of this unsighing people of the woods....

Here was a bare stage. In America there was a chance for a hero to stand forth, in Tocqueville's words, as "man himself, taken aloof from his country and his age and standing in the presence of Nature and God." In such a place the tenth child of a minor bureaucrat might fulfill a dream.

*For American romantics, of course, the reverse was true. They required a strange but old scene. In 1831 James Fenimore Cooper lamented the absence of romantic materials in America: "No annals... no manners... no obscure fictions... no gross and hardy offences." William Cullen Bryant, six years earlier, heard critics lamenting that his native country was "peculiarly barren of the materials of poetry." By 1860 Nathaniel Hawthorne knew where to find these materials—in Italy: "A poetic or fairy precinct, where actualities would not be so terribly insisted upon as they are, and must need be, in America... a country where there is no shadow, no antiquity, no mystery, no picturesque and gloomy wrong, nor anything but a commonplace prosperity, in broad and simple daylight.... Romance and poetry, ivy, lichens and wallflowers need ruin to make them grow."

Beltrami was not merely a European restless under legitimacy; he was also an intellectual deeply imbued with the philosophy of Rousseau. When Tocqueville spelled nature with a capital *N*, Beltrami would know what he meant. The American scene was not only new; it was, and was likely to remain, savage. Heroism does not prosper in a drawing room. It requires space and the opportunity for violence.

Like other Europeans of his time who felt suffocated under a surfeit of civilization, Beltrami idealized primitive life. The cult of the noble savage provided another impulse toward America, for there, it could be hoped, one might find simple people free of the shackles which in Europe bound men to a dead past and a diseased present.

Beltrami's worst disappointment in America was not the surly treatment he received from Long and his associates; he would have expected no better from men without "sensibility." His joy was clouded most by the degree to which the Indians failed to fulfill their assigned roles in the romantic scenario. He found them not the noble figures he had expected but, instead, "corrupt and degenerate . . . uncivilized, indolent and cruel." There was, of course, an explanation which could still preserve the purity of Rousseau's concept: *these* Indians had been corrupted by the presence of the traders among them. They had already caught the contagion of civilized life: the "red men who are most in contact with the whites are uniformly the worst."

Like Beltrami, many European painters and writers who toured the Great Plains could not record what they saw coldly, as anthropologists might. Many mixed passion with their paint. They were committed to the view that the ragged, treacherous, proud, simple, stone-age folk they found there must be somehow closer to a lost perfection than the people they left behind in Europe. They were not excited by "progress," that long effort to regulate human affairs by reason and custom so that the general condition might advance somewhat over the course of time. Even after he returned from America, Beltrami was still pursuaded that "civilized man is more barbarous than the savage."

Beltrami's ideal of primitive life established the background of his drama. It told him what he expected to find in America. And it required of him that he deal with the Indians in a way which he found in practice to be perilous. But such general concepts grouped themselves around a personal ideal more ancient and more demanding. Throughout his writings, out of the depths of his nature, he gives glimpses of an heroic attitude which is central to his story.

This view of life is that of the suffering hero. It arises from what might be called the Lancelot syndrome. There is a tradition of courtly love in European literature which probably originated at the court of Eleanor of Aquitaine in the twelfth century. That bitter woman had been married in her lusty youth to the pious Louis, King of France by birth and celibate by preference. She had, she said, "married a monk." When this alliance was finally dissolved, she was next married to an amply-passionate husband, Henry II of England, but he was eleven years her junior, and as she became older, he became distracted by a series of fresher companions. Ultimately, she and he parted company. Thereafter, in her court in Aquitaine, she had a sort of literary revenge against disinterested or disloyal men. She sponsored a series of poets in evolving stories of heroes who abased themselves to please the whims of their beloved. Lancelot was the chief of these men, willing to undergo any humiliation to secure the smile of his lady. Some of Eleanor's favorite tales told of his riding through the mud in a farm cart, permitting himself to be dishonored and unhorsed—all to prove his love.

There was in the spirit of the Middle Ages something which responded deeply and with delight to this image. Men took to suffering with a new alacrity, provided that it could be undergone under the gaze of a lady. There were tales aplenty. One told of three knights who received a blouse from a lady with the insane suggestion that the one who truly loves her will wear it alone with no armor in a tournament her husband is giving. Two "excused themselves." The third accepted, was badly wounded, but won her smile. German knights drank their own bath water and cut off their hands to please women, in a pattern of behavior which, if it seems incredible, is only a little more emphatic than some more recent cases. Let the reader be reminded of the words of Owen Wister describing the moment at which his "Virginian" finally breaks through Molly Wood's defenses: "He was not now, as through his long courting he had been, her

"Danse de Mariage chez les Canadiens," an eighteenth-century French engraving whose cheerful distortions exactly matched Beltrami's preconceptions of the Indians as a race of happy, contented, and altogether serene beings—an aristocracy of nature. The truth shocked him badly and left him more than a little bitter; the Indians he met, he said, were "corrupt and degenerate... uncivilized, indolent, and cruel," and while he took some comfort from the observation that such characteristics doubtless stemmed from contact with "barbarous" whites, his ever-important romanticized ideal had been irrepairably damaged.

half-obeying, half-refractory worshipper. She was no longer his half-indulgent, half-scornful superior. Her better birth and schooling had been weapons to keep him at his distance...."

The elements of this ritual have been fairly fixed since Eleanor gave to Chrétien de Troyes the *matiere et san*. The hero suffers for the love of a woman of higher station (in America, as Wister indicated, "birth and schooling" will do, though in Europe a title is to be preferred). The lady is married to someone else who is unworthy of her (or, at any rate, inattentive). And, to complete the oedipal picture, suffering gains him no consummation, merely a pallid smile, a perfumed handkerchief, a garter perhaps, or, at best, a tearful interview in a gazebo in which she takes his hand in hers and pledges that she loves him, but not, of course, in *that* way.

Beltrami's American journals are full of echoes of the literature of courtly love. The very form of those journals, his report on the dangers and disasters of "a poor, solitary traveler constantly contending against obstacles" was a series of letters to a "countess" whose mailing address and full name are not given. Later, the citizens of Bergamo in their memorial to him made it clear that she was, as Taliaferro had already learned, not his wife but the Countess Compagnoni, born Passari. We may be fairly sure that the Lady Julia after whom the heartshaped lake was named was no commoner. Beltrami was always proud of the fact that in his youth he had had the protection of the Countess of Albany, "the friend of Alfieri and Foscolo." In his mind there was always the face of the lady of high station, even while the mosquitoes bit, the Indians threatened, the boggy foothold sank. Always he was displaying his affections and his sufferings before women, but never did he abandon those principles of which he was so proud. He was celibate, he wrote, never carnal, for if he lapsed, the courtier-queen relationship would suffer. "Love," said Beltrami, "may be as pure and irreproachable as it is ardent and elevated." He would have no dalliance with "the beautiful Woascita," the elusive heroine of the "dreadful Bacchanals at Leech Lake." He was constant.

Such constancy to an ideal led Beltrami to include in the English edition of his *Travels* a dedication to womankind. He concluded that whatever doubts his critics might express of him and his medieval heroic stance, they "shall in nothing affect my worship for this adorable sex, nor even my last will. I bequeath my heart to woman; my soul to God; and the wicked to the D——."

Beltrami was not only an actor in a series of set pieces; nor was he merely a historian of those occasions. However absurd he may seem to be at first glance, he was a true hero. He insisted that history should occur in certain ways—with himself as the central figure. And he created his own opportunities for heroic action.

Men may behave well accidentally or in a sudden, unrepeated surge of vigor, but they deserve the name of hero only when they, like Beltrami, form an image of themselves and stick to it, forcing circumstances to accommodate to their ideal. The quality of heroic insistence is that strength which permits the long-sustained performance of a self-chosen role.

For Beltrami, it was that performance which occupied his mind; he was indifferent to the landscape except to the degree that it provided a backdrop. As a consequence, of course, he was a very poor observer and reporter. But, in his way, he saw more in the American West than did Long. That dutiful and cheerless man, with all his scientific instruments and his cadre of specialists, envisioned nothing, saw only what was immediately before his eyes. He could not imagine what men could do with such a setting. His portraits show him tight-mouthed and glowering; his writings reveal a crabbed mind, which never elaborated upon the data his travels presented to his joyless senses.

Long saw the West through eyes shuttered by Puritan expectations, finding in that undisciplined and generous environment the hostility of nature and the depravity of all habitations of men not yet brought under the reign of the elect. The effect of his predilection was to make him incapable either of self-conscious heroic action or of a vision of the West as the setting for prodigious things. Thus he was an unimaginative realist, constrained by the combined disciplines of the army and his New England background. Other men, however, might have arisen from the same sort of circumstances and become as capable of heroic and romantic insistence as Beltrami. Several, in fact, did. One such was Henry Hastings Sibley.

Chapter Three

Henry Hastings Sibley

Alexander Ramsey

I

IN THE SPRING of 1849, at the same confluence of rivers where Giacomo Beltrami and Stephen Long had struck up an instant and implacable antipathy, the two great public figures of the nineteenth century in Minnesota met for the first time. One was lithe, athletic, intellectual, upright, and rebellious. The other was heavy, phlegmatic, unreflective, morally compliant, and content with his times. Though of another tradition than Beltrami, Henry Hastings Sibley was a romantic frontiersman. Alexander Ramsey was a spoilsman-politician who became a frontier capitalist. Sibley's happiest years were spent among the Indians in a wilderness; Ramsey was as content in the sordid politics and commerce of the 1860s and 1870s as a rhinoceros in a mud hole. Sibley was a Jeffersonian Democrat; Ramsey a Grant Republican.

Ramsey was Minnesota's first appointed territorial governor, Sibley, its first congressional representative and first elected state governor. Ramsey became a powerful United States senator, then secretary of war; Sibley became, to his misfortune, a general. Ramsey was accounted by his contemporaries to be a great success; Sibley was thought a little strange, an eighteenth-century anachronism persisting into the Gilded Age.

There was a friendship between these two which survived many political confrontations and the reciprocal calumnies of their associates, a friendship which transcended dissimilarities of background, goals, and style, and which persisted for more than four decades, until Sibley's death in 1891. Every year when the two were near at hand, Sibley would call on Ramsey on the occasion of that first meeting in Mendota. Every year the arc widened between their divergent paths, but that friendship never snapped. On those annual visits they often sat together in heavy, high-backed, gray wicker chairs in the cavernous shadows of Ramsey's front porch, looking out upon the carriages passing toward one or another of the fat, fashionable frame houses in the neighborhood, where in their youth clumps of oak trees had sheltered Indian ponies and the black birds had sung beside the ponds. Their conversation was private. Neither has left to us an impression of the other, though Sibley was given to the writing of character sketches of his old frontier friends, and Ramsey, who survived him by a decade, had ample opportunity to memorialize Sibley in the fashion of the times. They had become accustomed to each other and learned to overlook imperfections, but perhaps neither wanted to look at the other as directly as portraiture requires.

Sibley was described by another contemporary as being six feet tall, rangy and muscular in build. His complexion was dark, "his eyes, with the iris rather small, of a dark lustrous brown, and of a kind, pleasing expression. . . . His hair was black, and in his earlier portraits he is represented as wearing a plain, black, closely trimmed mustache." He himself said that during his long hunts with the Indians, which sometimes took all winter, his beard grew shaggy. Clothed in rough buckskins stained with grease, blood, and sweat, with dogs at his heels, he looked like the frontiersman he was and wanted so much to be.

But he was no barbarian. Even in the beginning, when he made the long expedition from the American Fur Company's headquarters at Prairie du Chien (in southwestern Wisconsin) up the Mississippi to Mendota, he was an intellectual as well as an athlete, a man conscious of his education and his standing as satrap for the company over an area now occupied by large portions of five states. The journey to Mendota was through wild country, where he saw only one cabin in three hundred miles. It took two weeks to reach the cluster of huts which was to be his headquarters and his home for thirty years.

The position of a trader in this period was unlike that of the vagrant mountain man of the Rocky Mountain fur trade. A man like Sibley lived as might a feudal baronet, surrounded by whatever complements of civilization he wanted and could bring upriver by primitive craft from the outposts of civilization. Sibley had his books, "his horses and dogs and retainers to do his bidding," and soon after he arrived he began the construction of the large stone building which served as his warehouse, his office, a dormitory for his voyageurs, and his fortress. He was the representative of a company almost as powerful in his region as the government of the United States. He was justice of the peace for a region radiating three hundred miles from Mendota and the arbiter of disputes among Indians or settlers, receiving more deference than the commander of the garrison at nearby Fort Snelling. As the territorial population grew toward five thousand at the end of the 1840s, the old traders and some of the new settlers turned to him to organize the territory. He was their inevitable choice to serve as their delegate to Congress.

Sibley's biography progresses smoothly from this point, through his governorship, his military exertions against the Sioux, and his long gray years as a grand old man. But with his election as a delegate to Congress, that period in his life for which he had been prepared by training and inclination came to an end. When his letters and speeches and reminiscences are read and reread, it becomes clear that thereafter civilization closed in on him and he entered a world to which he was a stranger. That world was intended for men like Ramsey, not for the romantic refugee from puritanism that Sibley was.

Sibley wanted a life free of constraint, noble but uninhibited. The wilderness in which he wished to lead this life was the romantic wilderness, not the Judaic-Puritan wilderness. Why the distinction? Just as Beltrami and Long had seen the same river valley through different ideological lenses, so Sibley saw the forests and plains in one way while men still bound by a view of wilderness which he had rejected saw them in quite another. What he and they would do with wilderness was very different.

The same difference, it will be seen shortly, would appear in how they would treat its savage inhabitants. The Old Testament had taught the Puritans to think of wilderness as a desolation like unto Sinai, where a man could wander sun-crazed for days seeking water, hearing the wings of the kites flapping closer and closer. This was the image of the Great American Desert which was so strong in Stephen Long: a middle eastern image of baked, cracking earth left after the primordial deluge had receded, a desert surrounding the oases of prideful man, a wasteland stretching forbidding and reproachful to the horizon. With his mind on Sinai, a rabbinical commentator had said: "The earth . . . became mountainous as a punishment . . . and will not become level again until the Messiah comes." This view of wilderness was inherited from the rabbis by the men of the Middle Ages and from them by the Puritans.

In America the wilderness was the West. New England Puritans had biblical sanction for a gloomy view of what might be found out there. The rulers among them also had good economic reason to fear too much mobility and the absence of discipline. Cotton Mather called the West "the wrong side of the hedge." Michael Wigglesworth thought of it as a "devil's den . . . inhabited [by] hellish fiends." Timothy Dwight conjured up a population of "foresters . . . impatient of the restraints of law, religion, and morality." Edmund Burke had used the same key word, for he too feared what might happen when men were free of "restraint," but he could see not only foresters but also "hordes of English Tartars" on a vast steppe on which they would "wander without the possibility of restraint." Even Washington Irving (in his conservative phase) feared to see such nomads appearing on the western horizon ready to descend upon the settlements of those who had "gotten cattle and goods."

This admixture of political conservatism, religious paternalism, and capitalist concern for a ready, cheap labor supply was succinctly stated in the lament of Cornelius Felton in the 1830s, that the West was a place where there were "none of the restraints which fetter the characters of the working classes in other countries." Puritan fathers, like English Tories, feared that beyond the "hedge" there would beckon a licentious life which parishioners and working men might be unable to resist.

Henry Hastings Sibley, a "romantic refugee from puritanism," a man who attempted to take circumstance and shape it to his ideal.

Generations of young New Englanders did indeed set forth for the West, as others had left their villages for the city, in order to escape restraints. Though western migration was also propelled by overpopulation and encouraged by the exhaustion of rocky soil, it was often an alternative to revolt (an "escape valve," in an embattled phrase of Frederick Jackson Turner's). Escape to the frontier resulted from an explosion of those energies which could not be confined within the suffocating Puritan climate.

It is one of the extraordinary aspects of this escape that it had to be remade in each generation, as parents who had gone to the frontier were joined by Yankee compeers and in their middle age reinstituted some of the same constrictions from which they had fled in their youth. Thus Henry Sibley, the son of Yankee pioneers, escaped from the new New England those pioneers had re-created in Ohio and Michigan. He rebelled against the newly imposed constraints of which his father, Judge Solomon Sibley, was the chief guardian.

Solomon Sibley was born in Sutton, Massachusetts, six years before the Revolutionary War. He studied law in Boston and went west in 1795. After settling in Detroit, he rose rapidly to eminence: mayor, auditor, Indian commissioner, bank director, congressman, justice, and, finally, chief justice of the Supreme Court of Michigan. His fourth child and second son was Henry Hastings Sibley. A biographer provides the awesome catalogue of this child's puritan antecedents: the Sibleys arrived in the first shipments to New England, where

> in all matters of importance relating to the common weal, in church or state... [they] stand out as foremost figures. ...Their name is "Legion." They swarm. Sutton is their hive.... And all are interlaced and intermingled in a network of intermarriages, crossing and recrossing... with... other influential families... ministers, elders, deacons, church wardens, rectors, canons, bankers.... How thoroughly Puritanic this celebrated stock was is seen in the names transmitted to the children... among the antidiluvians Noah stands as prominent as ever... Abraham, Isaac, and Jacob... Reuben, Simeon, Levi, Joseph, and Benjamin

> ... Moses, Elijah, Joel, Amos, Jonas, Nathan, Nahum, Jeremiah, Isaiah, Ezekiel, and Daniel ...,

and so forth through Barak, Zerubbabel, and Rufus to the ladies, who included Tamar and Vashti. Sister Mary Sibley, it seems, was suspected of witchcraft in 1692 but was freed, though she did admit making cakes for the Indians.

The credentials of Sarah Whipple Sproat, Solomon Sibley's spouse, were just as compelling. She was the daughter of Colonel Ebenezer Sproat, who built a new *Mayflower* at the headwaters of the Ohio, down which he and his family floated to the mouth of the Muskingum, where a new town was founded. There Sarah was born and, in 1802, was married.

Her son Henry was a wild, rebellious boy. Sixty years later he said of himself: "I was more given to mischief than my fellows ... my dear mother often declared me incorrigible, and the black sheep of the family." He was given the best that the academy in Detroit could provide, then put under a tutor in Latin and Greek for two years and abided with increasing impatience the study of law. After two years he gave it up, longing, as he said, "for a more active and stirring life."

William Watts Folwell, president of the University of Minnesota, historian, and a friend of Sibley's in his later years, spoke of the young man as having "no stomach for the law or for scholastic or sedentary pursuits. His heart was with the Wild West."

Minnesota, Sibley thought, was unlikely ever to be anything but wild. He assumed, as did most of his contemporaries, that he would find there a permanent wilderness. Congressmen would dismiss it as "that hyperborean region of the Northwest, fit only to be the home of savages and wild beasts." Parkman would write of the "frozen northern springs" of the Mississippi, where "the fur-clad Indian shivers in the cold." And Sibley himself went there trusting that he had found a place beyond the reach of the civilized world: "I had no belief that Minnesota would become fairly well settled within fifty years. I had no faith in it as a farming country. I thought that the year 1900 would find it no better occupied than the country along the northern shore of Lake Superior."

Alexander Ramsey in the 1850s—the "shrewdest, sharpest, best politician in Minnesota," a man who altered ideals to fit circumstances.

Sibley recalled his wilderness years as his best. He enjoyed a condition of freedom and of dignity; he was respected, powerful, but unburdened. It was precisely the life he wanted:

> It may seem strange that men of education and culture, could be induced to endure the hardships, perils, and exposure, incident to the life of an Indian trader; nevertheless many such could be found among that class. The love of money was not the incentive, for rarely could or did a trader accumulate or become wealthy.... What constituted the fascination, it would be difficult to describe, except upon the theory that the tendency of civilized men, when under no restraint, is toward savagery as the normal condition of the human race. There was a charm in the fact that in the wild region, inhabited only by savage beasts, and still more savage men, one was liberated from all the trammels of society, independent, and free to act according to his own pleasure.

The young Sibley was, in William James's words, "an unencumbered man." His childhood had been a long rebellion, and now he was free. It is one of the fascinations of Sibley's career that he was not only a rebellious individual but also a good representative of a rebellious generation.

Sibley's contemporaries were engaged in a powerful reaction against puritanism. Theirs was a revolt of young Yankees against their ancestral burdens and a general passion for newness. Thoreau asked for "a spiritual molting season"; Hawthorne asked for a "busk," a ceremony in which society's old forms and devices would be thrown upon a bonfire and destroyed so that men could start afresh. For many, escape to the frontier was in itself a form of "busk." Sibley loved to quote old Leatherstocking, James Fenimore Cooper's hero, who found newness in nature "where he could ... open his heart to God without having to strip it of the cares or wickedness of the settlements.... Nature was a place to start fresh, where Herman Melville could envisage his heroes emerging naked each day into the "golden, glorious, glad sun."

Here is the romantic tradition in a new guise, Rousseau hybridized with German ideal philosophy. Jefferson had made the noble savage an honorary citizen of the new republic, and the New England transcendentalists set him "solitary in a wide, flat space" surrounded by the quiet humming of the Oversoul. Transcendental Nature was noble: it partook of the nature of God. Rousseau's Man was noble so long as he was free of the vexations, seductions, and restraints of city life. Man was good. Cities were evil.

Sibley accepted this doctrine and adhered to it all his life. As a middle-aged statesman, he lamented that the Congress had made preemption of land so expensive that "high rates of sale had forced thousands . . . to remain in the corrupting atmosphere of our large cities who otherwise would have become contented and happy tillers of the soil." He respected not only the happy yeoman on his farm but also men "who like Cooper's Leatherstocking are brought face-to-face with nature in her deepest solitudes." Daniel Boone joined Leatherstocking as the model for a whole race of frontier heroes, and Sibley could understand what lay behind James Perkins's description of Boone in 1846, as one who

> would have pined and died as a nabob in the midst of civilization. He wanted a frontier, and the perils and pleasures of a frontier life, not wealth; and he was happier in his log cabin, with a loin of venison and his ramrod for a spit, than he would have been amid the greatest profusion of modern luxuries.

There were, of course, few so heroic as to seek to live completely in accordance with the precepts of the Boone myth. The simple life was something which was accepted by many out of necessity rather than conviction, and it became progressively less simple when money could be found for comfortable complexities. Yet the vigor of the myth persisted, to be expressed in its full fervor by William Jennings Bryan as late as 1920.

By then, of course, it had become nostalgic, and it is in this late and rather rancid form that it appears to most of us in wild west novels and western films. In Henry Sibley's day it was an exhortation to a life of adventure.

J. Fletcher Williams gives us a picture of the young man sitting at the feet of frontiersmen of that older generation and listening to their tales. He was, says Williams,

> disposed ... to a life of close contact with the strange and romantic elements that have always given such a charm to frontier life in the eyes of the courageous and active.... His boyhood ... was passed in a region where every one of the old inhabitants was a fireside bard, reciting those wonderful epics of hairbreadth escapes and "accidents by flood and field," perils and feats of the half mythical heroes of the frontier, legends full of poetry and romance, well calculated to stir the blood and excite the ambition of the youthful listener. This largely accounts for the life he subsequently led....
>
> He listened to their stories of life in the great wilderness of the Northwest (so he once stated to the writer) like some tale of romance, filling him with a keen desire to see and traverse this wonderful land of lake, prairie and forest.

That Sibley was romantic does not mean that he was soft. He took the risks which his code required, seeking out exploits and wild companions, but he also assumed the no less hazardous responsibilities of a trader among savages. It was said that he was the best bareknuckle fighter in Wisconsin Territory and that he threw the wildest of the voyageurs at Mackinac out the door of his store. Williams reports a little gingerly that "some of the early settlers used to say that Sibley preserved order and discipline among his rough voyageurs by the actual use of the lash and bludgeon."

But it is also true that he held so strongly to his romantic idea of savagery that he took a view of the Indians which many of his contemporaries thought to be sentimental. When Charles Flandrau, another trader, read a dispatch that Sibley had captured three hundred hostiles and was about to hand them over for murder and rape of the settlers, he turned the paper over and wrote on its back, "He won't do it." Why not? He knew that Sibley and some of his friends were incorrigible in their belief that the Indian could be made into a useful citizen. This is no place to debate whether or not Sibley was right—to question what might have happened had the Indian been forced to make

St. Paul in 1851, as seen above, displayed the characteristics of a New England village and hinted not at all at the bustling metropolis it would become in less than twenty-five years under the persistent prodding of such hard-eyed speculators as Alexander Ramsey. Sibley, the consistent romantic, deplored the loss of this bucolic wilderness, but Ramsey, the realist and opportunist who tended to view the land in terms of quarter-acre lots, was doubtless satisfied to the bottom of his entrepreneurial soul by the transmutation he had played such a large part in bringing about.

an immediate change from his full pride as a hunter to a self-supporting farmer. The point is that there were many more men who agreed with Sibley in the 1840s and 1850s than we now like to recall. That reforming generation was convinced that since man is basically good (not, as the puritans held, a sinner perpetually seared by the wrath of an angry God), then, by adjusting institutions, man might be brought back to something like the bliss of his natural state. As optimists, they were naturally reformers.

No one has ever told well the story of the effect of the reformers of the 1830s, 1840s, and 1850s upon the Indian policy of the United States. That is a story well worth telling, but here it must be emphasized that the way in which men like Sibley accepted Jeffersonian and transcendental romanticism had profound effects upon their attitudes about the least urbanized, least civilized residents of the continent, the Indians of the Great Plains. Similarly, what they felt and said about the Indians tells us much about their view of themselves and how they wanted to live.

Many of the early Indian traders in Minnesota were well-educated men, convinced of the truth of Jefferson's ideals and of Rousseau's doctrine of the goodness of the "natural" man. They shared with Beltrami a presumption that the Indian, uncorrupted, was likely to be noble. It is remarkable how a long and intimate acquaintance with the real Indians failed to alter this view. After fifteen years of Indian trading, Sibley still spoke to the Congress of "the wild and noble savages who roam the western plains" and uttered a passionate plea for a humane Indian policy:

> The busy hum of civilized communities is already heard beyond the mighty Mississippi. . . . Your pioneers are encircling the last home of the red man, as with a wall of fire. Their encroachments are perceptible in the restlessness and belligerent demonstrations of the powerful bands who inhabit your remote Western Plains. You must approach these with terms of conciliation and friendship, or you must suffer the consequences of a bloody and remorseless Indian war. Sir, what is to become of the fifty or sixty thousand savage warriors and their families who line your frontier

> when the buffalo and other game upon which they now depend for subsistence are exhausted? Think you they will lie down and die without a struggle? No, sir; no! The time is not far distant when, pent in on all sides, and suffering from want, a Philip, or a Tecumseh, will arise to band themselves together for a last and desperate onset upon their white foes.

The time was more than a decade away, but then a new Tecumseh, Little Crow, punished the frontier with the most skillful and successful assault it had borne since Pontiac. It was Sibley himself who would lead the counterattack upon the Sioux, that "noble race" which, finally, in 1862, had gathered itself to break out of the wall of fire. But in 1850 Congress was heedless of his warnings. It was preoccupied with the problems of the black man and the white; it regarded a plea for the red race as a distraction.*

Sibley was no distant exponent of comfortable philanthropy, like the New England puppeteers of abolitionism. He lived among Indians for months or years at a time and was the father of a half-breed daughter. He married a "fine New England woman" in 1843, but he cared for his daughter and never disavowed the fullness of his participation in the life of the Indians. He recalled this kind of life, perhaps nostalgically, long afterward in describing an experience of an Indian friend after a battle when the two sides found ways to reconciliation: "The young warriors of the Dakotas made love to the Chippewa maidens and the Chippewa were by no means backward, in returning the compliment.... Old Leatherstocking would doubtless have been shocked... nevertheless, according to his old maxim, 'Human nature will be human nature the world over.'"

*Sibley had allies among the early Indian agents in the Midwest. Two who worked toward an Indian policy based upon his ideals were Joseph R. Brown, among the Sioux, and Jonathan E. Fletcher, among the Winnebagos. Fletcher arrived when "his Indians" formerly a "virile and prosperous" tribe in central Wisconsin, had been dispossessed and moved to Iowa, where they were being systematically debauched by traders. He followed them to two Minnesota reservations, each time to be forced out by land-hungry settlers. Despite the demoralizing effect of constant movement, Folwell says that Fletcher "induced many of the Indians to plant crops, to build houses... to have some of their children in school;... he did not succeed in getting any considerable number converted to the white man's religion, chiefly because it was so little commended to them by the white man's example.... They improved their farming, gambled less, and many of them abandoned whiskey. They framed and adopted a code of laws for their government. There is reason to believe that, could they have been allowed to remain on this reserve, within a lifetime they would have become nearly if not quite as civilized as the Indians of New York and New England." But the storm of wild rage which rose among the whites after the "Sioux Outbreak" drove them out of Minnesota. "Thus they pass beyond our horizon."

Sibley's own nature was an amalgam of romantic models. He drew these models not only from Cooper but from many of the same writers who contributed to Beltrami's assemblage: Thiers, Froissart, Malory, Scott, and the romantic poets. Sibley read about heroes both medieval and contemporary, molded his life after them, and was as careful as Beltrami that there was an audience. He did not take false postures, but he was acutely self-conscious.

For years he reported his own adventures for magazines like Porter's *The Spirit of the Times* and *Wildwoods*. As late as 1841 he left his post for five months and went on a foray with the Indians, "remained with the hunters, one of their number, assuming their dress, copying their manners, entering into their sports" and keeping careful mental notes. Here is a sample of one of his reports:

> I rode carelessly along, with but one barrel of my gun loaded, when, nearing the buffalo, he turned quick as lightning to charge. At this critical instant I had risen in my stirrups, and released my hold on the bridle-rein. The moment the buffalo turned, my horse, frightened out of his propriety, gave a tremendous bound sidewise, and alas! that I should tell it, threw Hal clear out of the saddle, and within ten feet of the enraged monster ... face to face with the brute, whose eyes glared through the long hair which garnished his frontlet like coals of fire, the blood streaming from his nostrils.... Holding my gun ready cocked to fire if he attempted a rush, I stood firmly, although I ... thought my last hour had come! How long he remained there, pawing and bellowing, I have now not the least idea, but ... at

Fletcher too, passes into the mists, replaced, as was Brown, by political hacks appointed by the incoming Lincoln administration. Typical of the traders who now appeared was Andrew J. Myrick, who refused Little Crow's women and children their rations, and, when told they were hungry, replied "let them eat grass." He was found dead early in the Outbreak, with his mouth stuffed with grass.

From the Minnesota outbreak, in 1862, until the Ghost Dance War a generation later, there were many who regretted that Fletcher and Sibley had not had their way. Of Brown, Folwell was to say: "The exigencies of party politics caused the retirement of Major Brown ... early in 1861; a calamity this, for the Sioux nation and for the United States.... Had he been left in office there would have been trouble enough awaiting him, but he might have succeeded. He might have induced many thousands, as he had many hundreds, of the Sioux ... slowly to assume the ways of civilized men. Had he not succeeded it would have been for lack of intelligent, consistent support and because of diabolical interference by white men without bowels and conscience. What Joseph R. Brown could not do with and for the Sioux Indians could not be done."

> last he turned slowly away, and I gave him a parting salute. ... The only one of the party within view now came up. I was so near the buffalo ... that my companion asked me if I had struck the beast with the barrels of my gun.

That companion might well have been Sibley's partner of many long expeditions, a half-breed hunter named Jack "Iron Face" Frazer. Sibley identified with Frazer, to an extent that explains who Sibley wished to be or thought himself to be—at least some of the time. Frazer was the subject of Sibley's only long literary work, a biography in which Frazer's adventures are often almost identical with those "Hal" reported as his own in the earlier magazine reports. In his biography of Iron Face, the author and subject tend to merge. A reader of that biography who also found Freud's biographical work intriguing might savor Captain Frederick M. Marryat's horrified comment on Frazer, whom he met on his American travels. He said of Iron Face that his chief ambition was "[to add] the scalp of his father." Marryat supposes that Frazer's reason was revenge for "the father's not having brought him up a white man." Sibley, at times, seems to have been sorry that his own father had.

Sibley's sending to eastern readers tales of his exploits in the West and his keeping one eye on the audience while the other was on the target apparently were not uncommon; the same self-consciousness was reported of other western heroes. Daniel Boone, the father of them all, survived by twenty-six years his first effusive biography. He was not, it is said, altogether pleased with it. Kit Carson thought that his chronicler, DeWitt C. Peters, "laid it on a leetle too thick" and later was embarrassed when, leading a search party, he found a worshipful account of his own career among the plunder taken by the Apaches from a wagon train. Davy Crockett, of course, wallowed in the adulation of crowds. As Henry Nash Smith has pointed out in discussing "Buffalo Bill" Cody, "the persons created by the writers of popular fiction were so accurate an expression of the demands of the popular imagination that it proved powerful enough to shape an actual man in its own image."

In the 1830s and 1840s scores of imitations of Cooper's forest romances were current and avidly read along with the medieval romances of Sir Walter Scott. These, too, were influential. Mark Twain wryly complained that chivalry, which had been interred with *Don Quixote*, was restored to life by *Ivanhoe*. It was the Louisiana State Capitol, with its Gothic turrets and finials, which provoked Twain's remark, but all the way up the Mississippi to St. Anthony Falls frontiersmen read "border ballads" and tales of chivalry, and laid up Gothic-revival houses. Sibley's friend, William Gates LeDuc, built the most ambitious castle in Minnesota, and in its parlor read *Ivanhoe* over and over again to his daughters. Sibley himself kept his complete set of Scott beside his Cooper, Hallam's *Middle Ages*, and Froissart's *Chronicles*.

Burke's picture of bands of buckskinned *condottieri* sweeping across the Great Plains, led by some new Black Prince or Gattamelata, was confirmed in some degree by the exploits of western outlaws. The armed horseman, free from the restraints of church and tradition, set loose in a strange and savage scene, did behave in America as he had elsewhere. To a generation which had been provided with a new stock of stories of brigands and banished knights, it was easy, also, to import into the Mississippi Valley ideals of behavior and, indeed, patterns of behavior drawn from the Age of Chivalry.

To take an extreme example: the propensity for dueling with weapons which was a part of the life of Andrew Jackson's old Southwest did not penetrate into the colder regions of the valley, but dueling in a new guise was demanded of men who would be leaders. Abraham Lincoln took on all comers in each forest hamlet he canvassed when he "wrestled his way into the legislature." In Minnesota, Sibley went through the same test. Folwell reports: "Endowed with a splendid athletic figure, he developed such skill and strength in the manly art of self-defense that, in the traditional words of a contemporary, 'there was but one man in the territory that dared stand up against him and that was 'Bully Wells.'"

It should not be thought that in the dust of a wrestling or boxing match Sibley abandoned his pride. He was no more an egalitarian in his direct relationships (whatever contemporary theory might have been) than was Andrew Jackson. Cooper, in his romances, always kept a clear distinction between the humble but heroic Leatherstocking type and the Oliver Effingham type, the gentleman disguised as a hunter. Henry Nash Smith has called this ideal "an indisputably upper-class hero." This was Sibley himself—descendant of the disguised Duke of Shakespeare's pastoral romances, the hereditary lord of Locksley Hall amid the merry men, Sir Wilfred of Ivanhoe amid the fellowship of the forest. Sibley thought of himself among the Indian traders, "that bold and hardy class of men, who despising the comforts and seductions of civilized life . . . fascinated by the unrestrained liberty of action offered by the trade with Indians . . . who, equally with honest Leatherstocking, shunned the society of [their] fellow white men, and above all, despised the whole machinery of the law. . . ."

Major Newsom, who knew Sibley for thirty years, spoke of him as "very jealous of his reputation." Folwell, another admirer, recorded the story of how French-Canadian squatters, who had occupied the site of the future city of St. Paul, elected Sibley to represent them when the land was finally offered for sale. As he proceeded to bid for it in his grave Yankee fashion, he was surrounded by a forest of clubs. His constituents stood by to dissuade any counter-bidder. "Sibley conveyed to each person . . . his proper area. . . . It was only after long delay and much persuasion that he could induce them to take their deeds. Ignorant of American ways, they felt their homes would be more secure in the hands of Monsieur Sibley, their ancient patron, than in their own."

This was not strange, since for many years he was the only civil magistrate in "a region . . . large as the Empire of France." While Nathaniel West writes so uncritically of Sibley that his truth cannot be fished out of his gush, he is probably right in saying that "the simple-minded people by whom he [Sibley] became gradually surrounded . . . were verily pursuaded he possessed . . . the high power of life and death. His word was the code imperial, his decisions unappealable."

On the one hand, there was the man who every year left his castle at Mendota to join Iron Face and the Indians in their annual hunt, who wrote "I allowed my hair to grow very long . . . and being bearded like a pard, and dressed in Indian costume, with two enormous dogs at my heels" looked like "a wild man of the woods." On the other hand, there was Sibley the conscious aristocrat, the man of (in Folwell's words) "dignity and grand manner," who almost failed of reelection as the representative of the territory to Congress because it was feared that he was too lacking in the heavy heartiness of congressional camaraderie to secure the concessions the settlers desired.

"Bluff Alex" Ramsey possessed all those convenient qualities Sibley lacked. Ramsey became governor, senator, and cabinet officer, while the surge of prosperity, settlement, and speculation which carried him upward were engulfing and destroying the frontier world which Sibley had sought. Sibley, however, performed his tasks conscientiously, leading his constituents with dignity down the road which opened before him. It was he who persuaded Congress to call the territory Minnesota and to select St. Paul as its capital. Counties and towns were named after him, though he was still young. As soon as the territory became a state and the inhabitants could have their own way, Sibley was promptly elected the first governor. But things began to go awry; his old Jeffersonian principles were not easy to apply, and his preference for a simple life in a sparsely settled country did not comport well with the requirements of a state which was doubling and redoubling its population each decade or with the predatory preferences of the speculators and land promoters. His prickly honor led him, as governor, first to fight a powerful railroad lobby seeking state underwriting for its bonds, and then, when ordered by the state supreme court to support the bonds according to the legislature's requirements, to heed the voice of the law and insist upon honoring the state's obligations even after the legislature had changed its mind. He was not reelected. The Republicans surged to victory in 1860, led by Ramsey, who had made a convenient switch from Whiggery.

The frontier, to Ramsey, was an invitation to exploitation, a vast tract of real estate which, when cleared of its wild animals, trees, and original inhabitants, would be ripe for development. To Sibley it was a lost Arcadia.

The Hawk that Hunts Walking, or Little Crow (the younger), chief leader of the great massacre of 1862, is seen seated at the left in this undated photograph.

II

IN AUGUST 1862, from Fort Abercrombie on the Red River to New Ulm at the crook of the Minnesota River, along a two-hundred-and-fifty-mile front, two thousand Sioux launched the first assault of the natives' Thirty Years War against steam engines, broken promises, agriculture, usury, breech-loaders, extortion, the telegraph, and civilization. In forty days they killed nearly five hundred of their foes and drove the farmers and traders back within the walls of forts and towns. They also demonstrated conclusively that theirs was a losing battle.

They could not win even against the dregs of civilization's forces left after thousands had been drained off to fight in civilization's own sort of fraternal warfare; they could not win despite their early success in effecting a surprise attack (the biggest news in the days before their assault was the appearance of new novels by Trollope and Hugo); and they could not win even under the leadership of a great warrior like Little Crow. When the American Civil War was over and veteran armies were let loose upon them, they still put up a good fight, but they never had a chance.

The task of defeating this first Sioux effort was meted out to Sibley, who had been their friend and companion. But their true antagonist, the organizer of their disinheritance, the proponent of their extermination, was Alexander Ramsey. While Sibley had been hunting with the Sioux and enjoying the unrestrained freedom of the solitary man, Ramsey was learning politics in a tough school, Pennsylvania. Pennsylvania had changed much since William Penn had said: "Oh, how sweet is the quiet of these parts, freed from the troubles and perplexities of woeful Europe." Two centuries of settlement and industrialism had created troubles and perplexities aplenty and had battened upon Penn's commonwealth a corrupt political system. Ramsey was a product of that system.

He had been orphaned at nine, had struggled to learn the law, was admitted to the Bar in 1839 and elected to Congress four years later, serving two terms. He was, by then, a thorough professional and ready for higher service to the Whig party. He could speak German to Pennsylvania Dutch farmers and talk tariffs with the local manufacturers. He became chairman of the State Central Committee and, after doing potent service to secure Zachary Taylor's victory in 1848, stood ready for his share of the spoils. Taylor was not slow in satisfying his friends; he replaced 540 of 929 presidential appointees and 6,200 of a total federal service of 17,780.

Ramsey aspired to be collector of the port of Philadelphia and was sorely disappointed when he was passed over for that potentially profitable post. He was given, instead, the governorship of Minnesota Territory.

When the new governor arrived, his province was a wilderness and his capital a squalid hamlet: "a dozen framed houses, not all completed, and some eight or ten small log buildings with bark roofs.... [It was] just emerging from a collection of Indian whiskey shops, and birch-roofed cabins of half-breed voyageurs." The population of St. Paul was about two hundred and fifty; that of the whole territory less than five thousand.

To Sibley's eye, the wilderness had been beautiful and, he hoped, permanent. Not to Ramsey. In his first message to a somewhat sceptical territorial legislature, he spoke of the vast country still under the control of the Sioux as "extensive, rich and salubrious... equal, in soil, to any portion of the valley of the Mississippi; and, in healthfulness, is probably superior to any part of the American continent." Then, in the ringing words of a prospectus: "It is known to be rich in minerals as in soil; is sufficiently timbered... watered by some of the finest rivers ... and is bespangled with beautiful lakes in every direction." He set about to secure that land for settlement, bringing in as his allies those Indian traders under Sibley's leadership who might be expected to oppose the liquidation of their own business, dependent as it was on the fruits of the wilderness gathered by the Indians themselves.

Ramsey, who had no interest in the flagging trade in pelts but could appraise a valuable tract of real estate, recognized that after the lush years of the early 1830s, the animals were becoming scarce, the traders more numerous, and the fashion for fur hats and trim declining. The traders had borrowed their stock

The Santee Sioux above, photographed in Washington in 1867, had appeared somewhat less civilized during the uprising of five years before. "They are to be treated as maniacs or wild beasts," General John Pope had said. Little Six, right, was hanged at Fort Snelling.

in goods from their companies, advanced those supplies to their best "producers" among the Indians, and hoped for a good hunting season in pelts to secure a return on their advances and pay off their loans. Hunting was increasingly more difficult, prices of fur lower, and the traders were in deeper and deeper trouble; since 1842 Sibley, by his own account, had lost ten thousand or more dollars a year. The only hope of recoupment was that the government would buy land from the Indians, who would in turn pay off their accumulating obligations to the traders. Sibley admitted that this would be enough "to set me on my feet and pay all my heavy liabilities for losses." Thus, for the first time but not for the last, the traders, whose influence with the tribes was great, were used to advance the interests of the land speculators (and, in fairness, of the settlers generally).

The acquisition of the Sioux lands in the treaties of 1851 was a sorry tale of extortion and undue influence. Ramsey presided over the whole affair, of which Sibley, it seems certain, was much ashamed (his authorized biography, written under the eye of the old man, never mentions the matter). One calloused observer remarked that "they were as fair as any Indian treaties." It seems very unlikely that much of the money reached the Indians after the traders and their agents, intermediaries, and sponsors got their share. More than $400,000 went immediately to the traders. More than a million dollars was to be set aside as a trust fund to pay for the twenty-five million acres acquired, but the Indians themselves probably obtained in cash no more than a cent or two an acre.

At one stage, Sibley was willing to forego his portion to complete the process, believing that a failure to conclude treaties after so much gold had been promised the Indians would lead to a bloody war; but a more general attitude was that of his rival, Henry M. Rice, who for a bonus offered to induce the assent of *his* client Indians. Authorized by Ramsey, Rice expended $5,173 in bribes, and the amount was charged against the Indian funds for "removal and subsistence."

By the 1851 treaties, an empire of rich agricultural land was "liberated from the hand of red savagery" and made ready for settlement, townsite promotion, railroad land grants, and speculation – in all of which Alexander Ramsey played a leading part.

A second province of a million acres was added to this empire in 1858 when the Sioux were bilked again, this time receiving something less than $85,000 after traders' claims had been satisfied. Those who have studied these treaties agree that their effect was to strip the Sioux of their ability to support themselves and to crowd them onto a ribbon-thin reservation along the Minnesota River at the mercy of Indian agents and rapacious traders. The Sioux had little recourse except to the violence of which Sibley had warned. Bishop Henry Whipple wrote to President Lincoln that the Indians had been swindled and were certain to resort to bloodshed, and that "as sure as there is a God, much of the guilt lies at the nation's door."

Humiliation and fraud worked to incite an Indian counterattack. Failure by the government to catch and punish Sioux outlaws who had massacred isolated settlers gave the impression not only of injustice but also of impotence. Refusal by local Indian agents to provide food to starving women and children detonated the eventual outbreak.

The long, slow, underequipped campaign led by Sibley to drive the hostile bands across the Missouri has often been reported. Our concern here is to show how he was used by Ramsey to visit upon the Sioux the wrath of those forces of civilization which he himself had distrusted, to carry out the military necessities caused by an Indian policy he had resisted.

Sibley accepted from Ramsey the command of the tatterdemalion troops which could be mustered to defend the frontier after most of Minnesota's best men had gone to fight the Confederacy. The Sioux had many hostages, the settlers were in panic, and Sibley's cautious prosecution of the war could gain him very few friends. Ramsey was constantly prodding him along, and after a few months Sibley was further embarrassed by the orders received from General John Pope, his new superior sent from Washington. Pope's titanic ego had been bruised by defeats on Civil War battlefields; he was desperately seeking a quick and dramatic success to restore his reputation. Both he and Ramsey insisted upon an extermination policy, which was not only beyond Sibley's means but was also blind to the necessity of keeping down the number of hostiles by weaning away Indians who could be induced to seek peace. Sibley, at the front, tried to save the lives of hostages by avoiding precipitate attack and the lives of his own men by wooing defections among his opponents.

After the first summer's successful campaign to drive the Sioux from the settlements, Ramsey told Sibley that "a feverish apprehension exists that you may be unable ... to protect our border settlements from the stealthy encroachments of the wily foe ... with a repetition of the dangers and horrors from which it was fortunately rescued last fall...." Despite Ramsey's rhetoric he had another worry: the loss of the lucrative trade with the British colonies along the Red River. The routes to those settlements lay just behind Sibley's advance posts, and perhaps, the governor suggested, a little more attention might be paid to them and a little less to the exposed and frantic settlements. He wrote Sibley that "the gold regions of the Saskatchewan and other portions of British America" were rapidly developing and the Hudson's Bay Company "have for a few years past been shipping to a great extent their annual supplies" by the exposed route. Therefore, he asked that Sibley dispose his forces with an eye to "the profitable trade which it will furnish our people, and our national pride." Sibley responded a little wanly, saying he was overextended already but would "open the communication referred to by you as speedily as I have the means to do so."

Ramsey got along very affably with Pope, who expected Sibley to terminate the unpleasantness with the Sioux quickly and neatly. The great man from Washington arrived as the first summer's campaign was nearing an end. He dismissed one of Sibley's battles as a "skirmish" and was miffed when Sibley addressed one of his dispatches to Ramsey instead of to himself. From his comfortable headquarters in St. Paul, he wrote the exhausted commander in the field, who was seeking to effect agreements with some Sioux bands: "It is idle and wicked, in view of the atrocious murders these Indians have committed, in the face of treaties and without provocation, to make treaties or talk about keeping faith with them. The horrible massacres of women and children and, the outrageous abuse of female prisoners still alive, call for punishment beyond human power to inflict. There will be no peace in this region by virtue of treaties and Indian faith. It is my purpose utterly to exterminate the

Sioux.... Destroy everything belonging to them and force them out into the plains.... They are to be treated as maniacs or wild beasts, and by no means as people with whom treaties or compromises can be made...."

Sibley replied, patiently, that he was endeavoring by delicate negotiations to detach those Indians who "had abandoned the fortunes of Little Crow ... to state to them that their friendly conduct in refusing to countenance or harbor Little Crow would be appreciated.... It would not do to precipitate matters now, for fear of alarming those who are coming forward to take their chances... it has been clearly proven that some of them even risked their lives in defense of the whites...."

Despite increasing pressure from Ramsey and other politicians who were conscious of the growing vigilante spirit on the frontier, Sibley persisted in seeking to distinguish between hostile and friendly Indians, and between those who had murdered isolated settlers and those who had participated in open warfare. Even after Pope's rebuke, he ordered his subordinates to "assure the Indians that it is not the purpose of the government to punish innocent persons.... You will of course prevent the men under your command from using any undue or unnecessary violence toward the Indians, should you take any of the latter, and especially do not permit any insult to the females."

Pope assured Ramsey that he was executing a policy in which they had agreed to place the Indians

> where they can no longer impede the progress of the settlements nor endanger the settlers. To treat all Indians (as the late outrages and many previous outrages have demonstrated to be the only safe and humane method) as irresponsible persons.... By this mode of treatment a great barrier ... will be at once removed, and the whole region to the Rocky Mountains will, in a very short time, be opened to emigration, travel and settlement.

By such pronouncements and by the distant exertions of field commanders like Sibley, Pope was confident that he could complete his chores on this sideshow campaign and return to glory in the South; in October 1862, he announced happily to

Major General Halleck in the War Department that "the Sioux War is at an end."

He was a little premature. Charles Flandrau, who was serving under Sibley on the frontier, wrote Ramsey a month later that Pope was "fatally mistaken." The settlers feared that Little Crow would return "from the west with reinforcements sufficient to reinact all the horrors of the past summer.... These fears ... may be regarded by General Pope and yourself as foolish ... [but] ... there is no peace. The whole country outside the lines of the troops is in the possession of the Indians. You, nor General Pope, dare not go 20 miles from St. Cloud without an escort of at least a company." In May of the following year Sibley wrote Ramsey that he was still short of men and supplies and that "we are in a state of war with the Sioux nation." Sibley spent the summer of 1863 leading an expedition against the Sioux across the Dakota badlands:

> If the devil were permitted to select a residence upon the earth, he would probably choose this particular district for an abode, with the redskins' murdering and plundering bands as his ready ministers.... Through this vast desert lakes fair to the eye abound, but generally their waters are strongly alkaline or intensely bitter and brackish. The valleys between them frequently reek with sulferous and other disagreeable vapors. The heat was so intolerable that the earth was like a heated furnace.... Yet through all these difficulties men and animals toiled on until the objects of the expedition were accomplished.

Pope had meanwhile retired, pouting, to a new general headquarters at Milwaukee.

Sibley had to contend with other difficulties, among the worst of which were mobs of settlers attacking his camps. Encouraged by politicians, these vigilantes wanted to execute all the Indian prisoners Sibley had captured. Ramsey was counseling President Lincoln (in jest, his daughter thought) to hang a few more Indians and increase Republican votes in Minnesota, and though Lincoln courageously insisted upon due process before hanging any prisoners, Sibley was charged with their protection and had to bear the wrath of the settlers. Twice he had to fight off lynch

Alexander Ramsey's house in St. Paul, an edifice whose gross eclecticism spoke for the man, is seen above; below is St. Paul in the 1860s, a fast-growing hustler's town that Ramsey could call home with conviction.

mobs. He was never to recover his popularity after being thus forced to demonstrate his refusal to treat all Indians as Pope and Ramsey would have him.

The end of the Minnesota phase of the Sioux War was reached when Sibley and General Alfred Sully drove the hostiles west of the Missouri and an uneasy truce was reached. (Later war was to be resumed again, further west, when Civil War heroes like George Custer had an opportunity to seek further bloody exploits there.) Sibley returned to private life, his public career, for all practical purposes, at an end. It seems doubtful that Ramsey failed to give some thought to the destruction that he would vent on his most potent rival for major political office by commissioning him for a military service that could not possibly enhance his public support. Ramsey was very quick to use Sibley in Indian emergencies, and knew his attitude toward the Indians well. Possibly Ramsey was just lucky in having so competent and so easily misunderstood a friend and rival. But he was usually too careful to permit history to evolve unaided. His training had occurred in Pennsylvania, where luck, in politics, was customarily arranged. On two occasions his lieutenants wrote him: "We have Sibley where we want him," and "We have succeeded in making a regular Sibley and Rice affair of it, with the Sibley party on our side. . . ."

But it may not have been necessary for Ramsey to be so full of guile. Sibley really had little appetite for public life in Ramsey's world. Even as early as 1850, when Ramsey had just arrived in the territory, the new politics had begun to replace the more seignorial style of the old frontier days. A friend noted that year that Sibley, upright and proud, had barely won a congressional contest in which his opponents had used "hope, fear, avarice, ambition, personal obligations, money, whiskey, oysters, patronage, contracts, champagne, loans, the promise of favors, jealousy, personal prejudice, envy—everything that could be tortured into a motive. . . ." That was Ramsey's arsenal, meticulously described.

In 1859 Ramsey succeeded Sibley as governor of the state, riding the tide of Republican popularity in the Northwest. He had survived a senatorial investigation of his handling of the Sioux treaties. Unabashed, he was often in Washington during his governorship, lobbying for land grants for railroads across the new territory. In 1853, he recommended to the territorial legislature that it ask Congress for additional grants and the next year succeeded in obtaining a legislative incorporation for the Minnesota and Northwestern Railroad, of which both he and his successor as governor, Willis A. Gorman, were incorporators. The assent of both the legislature and the Congress was necessary to reap the fruits of the treaties of 1853 and 1858. Ramsey's diary demonstrates the success of his efforts in the national body in the 1850s and the utility of early training in Pennsylvania political techniques; he offered Samuel Russell $5,000 in railroad stock for influencing Pennsylvania Whig members and $500 a head "to Colonel Carter for each Democratic member of Pennsylvania that should vote for the bill."

There were occasions when, even in those elastic times, such methods were not entirely successful. When a land-grant bill in which Ramsey was interested had a most significant clause altered to his advantage after the bill had been engrossed, the indignant Congress repealed the grant. They found that Colonel John W. Forney had altered the wording at the instigation of "someone not named." Ramsey was accused of being Forney's hidden principal in the affair, but the allegation was never proved.

Corruption was not a rarity in those years. In 1864 the state legislature elected Ramsey to the United States Senate, where he became a leading figure. Allan Nevins has characterized the Congress of those days as

> an auction room . . . a gallery where men interspersed patriotic platitudes with bids for sectional advantage, class advantage, above all the advantage of special interests. . . . the years 1868–73 were the years in which corruption kept pace with the upward curve of the business cycle; in which the lax morals of the financial world were transferred to the political world.

Ramsey managed to link these worlds, or to crossruff them. His diary shows the result; in 1869 he took his family for a summer's European junket and spent, apparently without much qualm, $7,477.45, while his mansion was being planned in the midst of one of his early additions to St. Paul. The St. Paul *Daily*

Press of February 5, 1871, reported that he paid twenty thousand dollars in taxes that year. During a two-year hiatus from major public office, during the mid-1850s, he wrote in his diary that he had multiplied his worth six times.

Ramsey's wealth and the use he made of it to influence legislation were of increasing interest to his constituents in the 1870s. Major Thomas Newson, a St. Paul journalist, asserted that "during the time Governor Ramsey held a state office, his salary never paid him for the amount he expended entertaining the legislature—and the governor says facetiously—'In the old days the members consumed an enormous amount of food.'" Ignatius Donnelly's newspaper, the *Anti-Monopolist,* implied that Ramsey and his supporters had spent thirty-two thousand dollars to influence the Republican caucus in 1869; a committee of the Minnesota House of Representatives presented a split report after an investigation of charges of bribery brought against Ramsey in seeking reelection to the Senate in 1875. Congressman William S. King, a politician sponsored by Ramsey, was charged with participation in the Pacific Mail Fraud of 1871, which involved bribery of members of Congress in the interests of subsidies for mail carriers.

Ignatius Donnelly made much of Ramsey's investment in the railroads, for which he secured land grants, and succeeded in persuading many Minnesotans that Ramsey was the local chieftain of the "rings," which many held responsible for panics resulting from speculation and which secured vast tracts of the public domain during the Grant Administration. Donnelly never was able to prove any malfeasance on Ramsey's part, though the senator did not trouble to disguise his interest in corporations which were the beneficiaries of legislation he sponsored.

Ramsey's views on matters of broad public policy earned him the antipathy of reformers, who were already confident that he was using his public power for private speculation. He was one of the band of stalwarts who surrounded and used Grant. A frequent dinner guest of the president (though he criticized the White House cuisine), Ramsey had voted to convict President Andrew Johnson during his impeachment proceedings and called Grant "a first-class president and trusted Republican."

Like his close friend Senator Zachariah Chandler and Chandler's chief allies, Oliver P. Morton and Roscoe Conkling, Ramsey fought against reform of the civil service. He was always ready to "wave the bloody shirt" to prevent amnesty for the defeated leaders of the South, predicting that if Grant were beaten by Horace Greeley in the election of 1872, Jefferson Davis would be appointed secretary of state and that other high positions would be filled by officers of the rebellion.

Major Newson, writing when Ramsey was at the peak of his power, described him thus:

> The shrewdest, sharpest, best politician in Minnesota today, is Alexander Ramsey... jovial, bluff, off-hand.... No matter whether these elements of character are affected or genuine, they are... parts of the man.... He has great command over his feelings and can greet an enemy, especially if he has any point to gain, as cordially as his best friend; indeed, in such a case, he is a good deal more than cordial. This arises not from policy, but from total forgetfulness of any political injury done him.... One of the great and strong points in his character is his non-committalism, especially before election.... He... makes everybody think he is a personal friend... and in case of a sudden rumpus you will always find him missing. When he gets into trouble, however, he is like a steamboat, backs out gracefully.... He is a liberal in his religious views, if he has any.... Many interesting incidents of the method Mr. Ramsey has adopted to quietly slip through the world with the least possible friction, might be given.... One of his peculiar traits is this: while a dozen small-fry politicians are fighting for the spoils, Ramsey is in the corner enjoying his political repast, and when the battle is over he smacks his lips and cooly remarks —"Well, I can't see what all the fuss is about."

Ignatius Donnelly, an early ally of Ramsey's and later a dedicated foe, called him "cold-blooded, secret, deceitful, and cruel." Donnelly was heading for Populism while Ramsey was taking his seat among the stalwarts of the Grant Administration; perhaps, therefore, a more temperate view might be that of a regular Republican, Governor Horace Austin: "As to the means that he will use to secure [an] end there can be but one question with him, and that is whether those means... tend to promote his purpose. That is a fair indication of my opinion of Alex Ramsey as statesman, moralist, and philosopher." William H. C. Folsom, the area's first major historian and a colleague of the young Ramsey, reported Ramsey as "hale, hearty, and well-preserved . . . genial and pleasant in his manners, and would impress the ordinary observer as one . . . who is the happy possessor of a good digestion, a serene temper, and clear conscience."

Ramsey's power in Minnesota was brought to an end by the same forces which created it: machine politics. He was getting older, and there were new men on the scene who coveted power. He was in the way. In 1875 a combination of ambitious competitors narrowly defeated him for renomination. He had been in the saddle for nearly twenty years, undisputed as the master of the Republican party.

Though he lost his political base in Minnesota, Ramsey still had friends in Washington. He was appointed to President Hayes's cabinet as secretary of war. He did not, however, permit such posts to distract him from his central objective, getting richer. A recent historian, John C. Haughland, has concluded that business was his first love and his last. He died in 1903, rich in honors and possessions.

There are some men who are born at the right time, fitted to prosper according to the requirements of the day. Alexander Ramsey was one of them. Neither compunction nor remorse distracted him. His attitude toward the Indians was that of most of his contemporaries, and his readiness to exploit his friendships was typical of his times and his profession. When an associate said that Sibley was exactly where they wanted him—in the perfect place to serve their interests—Ramsey saved the letter but not that of any remonstrance in reply.

Ramsey, rich and content, was accounted a success. Sibley, in the last thirty years of his life, was out of harmony with his surroundings. His tattered band of old frontier friends and his odd affection for the Indians made him suspect. Despite the honors rendered him, he was an outsider. In his old age he reflected on the changes which had transformed Minnesota's wilderness into a rich agricultural and industrial area. Its population, in the time he had known Ramsey, had increased from five thousand to more than a million. He, too, had prospered, albeit more modestly than Ramsey, but to him much had been lost. "To an old hunter like myself, accustomed to the solitude of forest and prairie, these changes are . . . not unattended with the lingering regret which we feel when some fair but wild vision disappears suddenly from our enraptured view."

Ramsey in 1900, a lifetime of scrambling after the main chance written in his face.

Chapter Four

Harvey Ellis

Daniel Burnham

I

At the end of an hour we saw a far-away town sleeping in a valley by a winding river, and beyond it on a hill, a vast gray fortress with towers and turrets, the first I had ever seen out of a picture.
"Bridgeport?" said I, pointing.
"Camelot," said he.

THERE IT WAS, the capital city of Mark Twain's Middle Ages. There loomed up the pennanted towers, the greensward, and the moated keep; there strolled the knights and damsels. However strange it may seem, Sam Clemens, the son of Hannibal, the youth of Virginia City, the bridegroom of Elmira, and the bourgeois of Hartford, walked in imagination all his life with Joan of Arc, Gawain and Arthur, with princes and with paupers. But it is not strange to those who know, not Hannibal (it had not the means), but St. Joseph, St. Louis, St. Paul, Minneapolis, or Menomonie. There, from far away you may still see vast gray fortresses with towers and turrets, with barbicans and keeps, their round-arched entries garlanded in limestone ornament, their pinnacles bearing pennant staffs. These are buildings of which John Wellborn Root said, their "only lacking detail is a shriveled head thrust over the cornice on the end of a pike."

In the American mind of the 1880s there was a strain of fantasy, which Mark Twain put into medieval romances and Harvey Ellis put into architecture. Ellis was the greatest American architect of fantastic medievalism, and for a decade he had the opportunity to create, on the bluffs above the slow, brown rivers of the Middle West, castles, keeps, and tombs. He made vast piles of masonry, not just replicas of ancient example but new creations in the spirit of an imaginary chivalric age.

For ten years, in these river-ports-becoming-railroad-depots, Harvey Ellis found clients willing to accommodate themselves to his visions. They commissioned him to sketch his visions and rejoiced as sketches were made tangible in pink Luverne jasper, Portage Entry sandstone, or Missouri limestone. For a while they lived in them, without embarrassment, thinking them perhaps a legitimate expression of the pride of a generation that had defeated the aborigines in bloody battle, conquered a hostile climate, and had come to have, in their own baronies, the power and the purse to express very expensive whims.

Then, in 1893, a blight fell upon the land. Crop failures coincided with an international financial crisis. Confidence was lost. The economy of the region passed through a long depression; local firms increasingly fell under the control of distant financiers, and architecture reflected a new restraint, a new reluctance to display color or verve; even after prosperity returned, caution persisted. Consolidation of the economy brought deference to bigness, a willingness to sacrifice vitality for ordered magnitude. A failure of nerve in architecture brought deference to cool, classic precedent. Harvey Ellis, meanwhile, was reduced to putting his fantasies on canvases he gave away to friends.

Until very recently it would have been impossible to tell much about Ellis, the great architect of fantasy. A few rather patronizing essays about him can be found in the trade journals, an affectionate memorial chapter in a book by the essayist and architect Claude Bragdon. Little else. Ellis was a vagrant, irresponsible alcoholic. But as researchers accumulate the evidence, it now appears that he was much more.

What Bragdon and his colleague Francis Swales said of Ellis was based upon their acquaintance with him in Rochester, New York, during a few years before his death in January 1904. Ellis said that his deceptively sturdy appearance came of being "pre-

Harvey Ellis in 1900. His sturdy appearance, one critic maintained, came of being "preserved in alcohol for twenty years."

served in alcohol for twenty years," but by then he had stopped drinking. He had gray eyes and a sweeping moustache, talked incessantly, but never about himself. He knew by heart Froissart and Malory, the Icelandic sagas, the tales of the Brothers Grimm. His paintings (now collected in the palace of Mrs. Homer Strong, in Rochester) are medieval in subject and spirit, flat in plane, story pictures of knights and devotional pictures of saints and angels and of the Madonna. He had become a Roman Catholic and composed his religious pictures without the saccharine qualities esteemed at the time; his were cool, impeccably composed.

Dressed in a robe that might have been Japanese or of a priestly order of which he alone was a member, theorizing interminably about architecture and art, he would turn out illustrations for sale to *Scribners* or *The Craftsman*, but his paintings were not for sale.

Bragdon says, "He could not endure the patronage of the wealthy buyer while if a true connoisseur expressed a liking for one of his pictures, Harvey usually insisted on making him a present of it." Swales says that "he permitted himself to be continually cajoled into giving away his sketches, and even drawings, paintings, and etchings upon which he had spent several days' or weeks' time." He had virtually abandoned architecture and was so secretive that Bragdon never knew how much he had accomplished in the West. "He never discussed his personal affairs, they seemed scarcely to interest him. . . . The only things he seemed to care for were to paint cryptic, unsaleable pictures, under a still north light, with plenty of time and plenty of cigarettes, and to talk about anything under the sun except himself to anyone who would listen."

This was not the Harvey Ellis of his great days as an architect. Then he was not so respectable. In his thirties, according to an old friend in Rochester, "he won every big competition there was, but never for himself. Whenever the competition was announced, the first architect to find Harvey in a saloon would pull him out, sober him up, set a draftsman beside him until he finished the drawings, give him some money, and turn him loose again." That was how it was in St. Paul, St. Joseph, and St. Louis. Bragdon heard that "he never knew what salary he was getting.

When he found his pockets empty he went ... for more money, and got it."

Ellis wandered from city to city, winning national acclaim for J. Walter Stevens in St. Paul, then for Leroy Buffington in Minneapolis, then for Edmund Eckel in St. Joseph and George Mann in St. Louis.

The *Western Architect*, reviewing this period, said: "The drawings and designs of the late Harvey Ellis ... came just short of influencing western work more strongly than that of any other designer, before or since his time.... Circumstances ... conspired to prevent him from carrying out his designs under his own name.... No one else could do such striking things and yet avoid the bizarre."

Bragdon, who also defended the reputation of Louis Sullivan during the long years of *his* disgrace, sought to redeem Ellis as well: "Harvey Ellis was a genius.... Had it not been for the evil fairy which seems to have presided over his birth and ruled his destiny ... he might have been a prominent instead of an obscure figure in the field of American art; but even so, he exercised an influence more potent than some whose names are better known."

There are those who believe he had a hand in the development of the ornament that made Louis Sullivan's office famous and others who have written that his was the design that won the competition for the Cathedral of St. John the Divine in New York for Hiens and La Farge. It seems probable that the St. Louis railroad station, a masterpiece ranking with any of Henry Hobson Richardson's buildings, was a product of the intelligence of Harvey Ellis. In this instance as in others, Ellis probably came in either during the competition to put his touch on the drawings or afterward to revise them into what was essentially a new and better building. The record architect for the building, Theodore Link, was a competent but pedestrian designer, and he broke a classicist pace at this time very briefly. Afterward, once again, Link got new clients and Ellis went back to the gutter.

Ellis was born in 1852 in Rochester, New York, the son of an upstate politician. Family correspondence indicates that before he was twenty he was an anxiety to his mother, who constantly adjured his younger brother, Charles, to try to set Harvey upon a straight course. In 1870, to the relief of all, he won admission to West Point. But he was dismissed after a year, the records attributing his failure to a weakness in French, family lore attributing it to a weakness in chastity—he was said to have achieved a liaison with a lady, perhaps an actress, whom he secretly married.

There is some evidence that he was sent abroad to forget the lady. (Ninety years later his niece said that his father had had the marriage annulled while Ellis was in Europe; other draftsmen who knew him said he had studied there.) Scraps of sketches of European monuments, drawn in Harvey's hand upon the back of Express Company documents, were found in Buffington's archives; an essay on the architecture of Venice, reading like a briefly dutiful son's report to his father, was scrawled upon a Rochester photographer's stationery and kept in the family papers. (It is difficult, even so long after his death, not to call Harvey Ellis by his first name. He said that everyone did except one office boy: "that one called me Harve!").

He was back in Rochester by 1875, for his mother was imploring his father through the mails to find something for him to do. He was already known as a rakehell in town. In the spring of that year Ellis was sending to his brother Charles for help in securing his trunk from his parents, who had moved to Albany. Their communications with the prodigal had been so completely severed that in August, when his father was in New York on a business trip, he spotted a familiar, tall silhouette against the window at the far end of an engineer's office on lower Broadway and was startled to discover that it was, indeed, Harvey. He reported to his wife, that their son had been "steady" (on the wagon) for some months and looked well. In 1877 and 1878 he joined the Albany office of Richardson while that huge atelier was at work upon the city hall and the state capitol.

In February 1879 Harvey, once more taken in hand by Charles, was back in Rochester, where for the next five years they turned out scores of designs for buildings constructed throughout western New York and Pennsylvania. Those that can be identified today are modest commercial buildings, schools, small-town hotels, and some well-disciplined "Queen Anne" houses. There is no need here to jump into the critical broil about Louis Sullivan's work of this period, but it is fair to say that Ellis's compares with it very favorably.

He was developing, within constricting budgets and among constricting clients, those skills that led one of Richardson's admirers, Hugh M. G. Garden, to say of Ellis that "he was a master of composition, both in his drawings and his designs of buildings, and probably no one in his time approached so closely to Richardson in the quality of his work."

Ellis was without opportunities in Rochester to build the vast buildings that filled his imagination. Richardson had found clients in Pittsburgh and Chicago, and Louis Sullivan was finding them, too. Ellis looked to the West for "opportunities . . . to design for the use of rough-hewn materials in great, picturesque piles." He had won a national design competition for a tomb for President Grant in 1885 but was probably not discouraged from leaving Rochester by his family, which was embarrassed by his debauchery and his predilection for women not considered respectable.

He was already known in the West in the circle that included Sullivan, Frank Lloyd Wright, and George Elmslie; a later associate of theirs, William Gray Purcell, said that Ellis's name was "well known to everyone who read an architectural magazine from 1880 to well past 1900." It is known that Ellis departed for the West in 1885, but thereafter he used every possible device to baffle biography: false names, disappearances, purposeful anonymity, sheer vagrancy. We do not know whether or not he stopped in Chicago to work with Sullivan; several Rochester publications say he worked in Chicago, and some of the Auditorium Building ornament looks like his. It is possible that he returned to Chicago to do some commissions in 1899. At any rate, a Sullivan student, Thomas E. Tallmadge, wrote in 1908: "An ideal artistic atmosphere pervaded the colony in the old lofts of Steinway Hall. . . . the little band of enthusiasts who had raised their feeble standard of revolt against the disciplined ranks . . . Perkins, Wright, Spencer, Myron Hunt, George Dean, Birch Long, and with them . . . associated in spirit if not in person . . . was the gifted but irresponsible genius, Harvey Ellis, poet-architect, whose pencil death stopped ere it had traced more than a few soft lines of his dream of beauty."

Much of Ellis's work displayed his fondness for things medieval. Above is the Samuel C. Gale house in Minneapolis, reared in 1888 and razed in 1933. Below is a typically fanciful drawing of the entrance to a Minneapolis subdivision — done under the alias of "Albert Levering."

Elmslie said he knew Ellis, but denied any association with the Sullivan office. Purcell, Elmslie's partner in later years, dismissed the question as beyond proof, saying of Ellis, "A very great architect, . . . before LHS [Sullivan], before Wright, . . . paying fealty to none, . . . in my view greater than Richardson. . . . You have a man to appraise who stands on his own feet."

That appraisal is easier to make in St. Paul than in Rochester. In Minnesota, for the first time, Ellis found clients who would let him build his castles. Even his commercial buildings grew larger, more daring. He required an extravagant budget, but he could work wonders. For John L. Merriam, banker and real estate promoter, he designed a gigantic red sandstone fortress-residence, which stood until recently on a hill overlooking the state capitol. Its great hall was composed of rose marble and Spanish leather and fruitwood and stained glass. There was a gold and ivory dining room and a parlor whose wall of mahogany was covered with the Celtic interlaces of illuminated manuscript. The disentangling of influences is impossible in this period. Richardson's great Marshall Field warehouse store influenced everybody; Harvey Ellis's Noyes Brothers and Cutler warehouse of 1886 have solemnly been said to have been modeled on Sullivan's Walker warehouse, though it was built two years earlier than Sullivan's work. What is important is to give Ellis and his clients their due: his Germania Bank Building, designed for Stevens, is still St. Paul's most impressive tall structure, and in 1887, he and Leroy Buffington made a major contribution to architectural history.

Buffington was canny, prolific, and litigious and knew a good colleague when he saw one. He had been practicing a disorderly "Queen Anne" before Ellis's arrival and relapsed into a plodding classicism after his departure. But while Ellis was in his office, he enjoyed a national reputation, which has persisted to some extent to this day.

After a lifetime of litigating for the right to be known as "the father of the skyscraper," the old man admitted that the design of what he called "the world's first tall steel frame office building," a twenty-nine-story structure to be built in Minneapolis in 1887, was Ellis's work. The sketches that served as Buffington's basis for claiming royalties for later skyscrapers were almost certainly from Ellis's hand. Purcell said of this building that "in being a unit from sidewalk to roof, ... [with] no forced values in the general design treatment to make it appear as if of solid masonry," it anticipated Sullivan's Wainwright Building of four years later.

In 1891 Buffington published an Ellis sketch of a bank building.* It was to be a jewel box, sixteen years before the first of Sullivan's fine small banks appeared. A rich terra-cotta frieze anticipated the sculptured ornament of the Prairie School. Blank walls would keep out noise and dust; fans would supply air, and electricity, light. A frieze of figures, an elaborately arched entry, and Moorish niches all provide a clear anticipation of Sullivan's Transportation Building of 1893 and of Sullivan and Elmslie's Owatonna bank of 1907.

Buffington, said Bragdon, "gave Harvey, at the end of every day, amounts varying from a quarter of a dollar to several dollars, and, whatever the sum, in the morning it was gone." Ellis gave Buffington a succession of designs more powerful than anything that crafty manager could ever produce for himself. In Menomonie, Wisconsin, for example, inside a heavy sandstone fortress called the Mabel Taintor Memorial Building (1889), there is a small theater of fiery stained glass and fanciful screens, its walls gilt and stenciled, its colors still glowing, and its plan pronounced by a recent professional critic to be "beautifully designed." In Minneapolis, Pillsbury Hall still dominates the University of Minnesota campus. Another Ellis design, Nicholson Hall, is nearby.

This was the time of Ellis's greatest achievements. In city after city his sprees were financed by architects and clients for whom his imagination conjured up marvels to be made into stone. Alcohol loosened his compositions, but they were grand. Here is a contemporary description of the interior of a house designed by Ellis for Samuel Gale in Minneapolis:

> Off the hall and partially separated by Moorish screen work is an alcove divan. On one side is an alabaster and mosaic

*The original drawing, probably done in 1888, is in the Buffington Archive at the University of Minnesota; Buffington removed Ellis's signature for publication.

> mantel extending from the floor to the wooden-beamed ceiling. At the central point will be a beautiful silver plaque. ... The entire hall will be wainscoted to the ceiling in oak finished to a pale amber green.... The library and morning room are finished in mohogany with elaborate plaster ceilings.... The drawing room is white and gold, with a ceiling of pale yellow silk with a pattern of plush of a pale blue appliqued thereon ... the pattern emphasized with silver-headed nails....

There was nothing of the "Brown Decades" here. Throughout Ellis's work, even in the final years of his discouragement, he celebrated color, dancing mosaics, jeweled stained glass. He was, in this respect also, a colleague of Sullivan, Elmslie, and Wright.

From 1888 to 1893 Ellis divided his time between Minneapolis and Missouri. For Edmund Eckel and George Mann in St. Joseph he did another German-American Bank, many residences and warehouses, and a police station. Later, for Mann alone, he designed houses, a hospital, a water tower, park entries, and the city hall in St. Louis.

He was marvelously dextrous in composing variations in the style of Richardson or Richard Morris Hunt, or even the British architect, Charles Voysey. Ellis obviously knew Hunt's work, but his own was less scholarly and more bizarre. He also began to import certain southwestern influences derived from the Spanish baroque. Perhaps he made a trip to Texas and California. There is evidence that he did. His disappearances were longer. His alcoholism seemed to be deepening. Then, in 1894, something happened. He left the West and returned to Rochester.

Perhaps by this time the economic depression was being so strongly felt that Ellis no longer could find the clients for his exuberant fancies. Perhaps it was at this time that he underwent his religious conversion. His allegorical paintings and some of his later writing indicate a deep and almost morbid sense of sin, and his propensity for escape from the vulgar, clamorous world may have found a new route. Ellis was never heroic in a public arena. But he was capable of making a sharp break, of radically altering his life. Swales merely tells us:

> Realizing that all was not going to his satisfaction, he broke away from the habits and acquaintances which he had cultivated to his disadvantage and returned east to seek some quiet nook where he could work in peace and be away from roistering friends.

Bragdon puts the event somewhat more directly:

> On a certain day of a certain year he rose from his besotted bed and for a period of ten years did not touch alcohol until, a few months before his melancholy death, weakened by disease, he sought its aid to give him strength for his daily task.

The nature of his crisis of 1894 will never be known, but it is possible to reach some general conclusions about his character. Ellis was a romantic artist, without the strength that men like Wright and Purcell drew from the deeper philosophic levels of the romantic tradition. He created fantasies in architecture and in painting (and his late paintings often included buildings like those he had built in the West). His eastern friends wholly misunderstood these fantasies and their relationship to the life and architecture of the West. Swales thought, for example, that the West in the 1880s

> probably lacked at that time, certain amenities essential to the well-being of the thorough-going artist that Ellis was. Among them, competition, intelligent and appreciative criticism and honest understanding of his endeavors. He was consequently almost wholly without companionship of men of his own intellectual class during his long sojourn in the prairie cities and except when "buried" in producing some fanciful decoration or architectural design was depressed and unhappy. However, he kept that so well concealed beneath an always apparent good humor and flow of bright comment that few, even of his intimates, suspected it.

In his generous effort to imagine the conditions under which Ellis "probably" worked, Swales, moved both by friendship and

The Mabel Tainter Memorial in Menomonie, Wisconsin, is probably Ellis's best-known building—and surely one of his most impressive. Seen above is the arched entranceway of the building, whose elegant intricacies were carried throughout the building's exterior and interior.

ignorance, portrayed a man of taste and talent lavishing his gifts, unappreciated, upon a wasteland. In fact, however, Ellis did very well in the West until the depression of 1893 discouraged those who had been his patrons and the eastern cult of classic propriety in architecture triumphed over the romantic and innovating spirit of the 1880s, of which he, Root, and Sullivan had been the leaders. The spread throughout the West of a "uniform ceremonious style," after Daniel Burnham's Roman triumph at the Chicago Exposition, left no opportunity for a man with a gift for fantasy and a disdain for dullness. It was not western barbarism but eastern philistinism that blighted Ellis's career as an architect.

The West in the 1880s was fertile in ideas and architectural innovation. There was plenty of "competition, intelligent and appreciative criticism." Professional architects and amateurs were enjoying an extravagant opportunity to build whole cities in that decade. The architectural sketch clubs, which flourished in all the major western cities, nurtured greater vitality, better talk, and stronger commitment to architecture as a living art than was to be found in the exhausted, sluggish, and inhibited architectural communities that settled in the great eastern centers after the deaths of Richardson and Stanford White. The draftsmen of the West were minnesingers of the graphic arts. They maintained a vigorous gypsy community—witty, irreverent, and contributing joyous preparation for the achievements of the Prairie School.

Ellis was first among them in technique and in design. But he was no more a part of their boisterous camaraderie than he had been a member of the artistic community of New York. He was a loner. He was always engaged in a furtive rebellion against authority and bourgeois society.

Bragdon thought Ellis mysterious, "the most impersonal person I ever encountered," and there is no question that he was evasive. There is strong evidence that in his last years he adopted a role, derived from his reading of medieval romances, and that was the role of the jester. His wit was famous, his irreverence feared. In an essay that appeared in *The Craftsman* shortly before his death, Ellis wrote of the life of one "who feels keenly, ... whose only weapons are words of which the sharpness may glitter and play, but must never strike."

Often he wrote or drew parodies. An "Albert Levering" sketch published in 1904 looks suspiciously like Ellis parodying his own idiosyncrasies of draftsmanship, and a few years earlier he produced a ponderous, earnest, and mawkish essay on Bragdon for the "Brochure" series, which reads so much like Bragdon (who had no sense of humor) that it has been taken "straight" by the critics. Bragdon, he says, was

> a model of deportment, of a character absolutely without blemish, ... quiet and unaffected, reserved ... difficult of access, yet when well known one of the most lovable of men, as well as one of the purest minded, ... always to be found [among] the little bands of admiring friends and disciples, listening for the never-wanting epigram or the clarifying sentence that solves ... Schopenhauer's place among the philosophers, parlor-magic, the color in the works of Tieapelo [sic], or the acceptability of the atomic theory ... he lived the life of a healthy, normal boy.

Bragdon, who would have loved this description and seen nothing glinting within the velvet, had written a faintly deprecatory essay on Ellis for the same series, saying of Ellis that some of his work was "too fanciful, too exuberant ... while others halt and render their elusive ideal actual, he presses onward toward a new ideal, like a child who deserts its doll to chase a butterfly."

Bragdon's piece was too much for Swales, who thought him "a very *superior* friend." He told Ellis it was "rotten." Ellis replied: "Well, I've written an article about *him,* and I have described him as a 'young man of *model deportment*'!" To Ellis, growing up like a "healthy normal boy" was to grow up dull, and Swales went on to point out that, "several years passed before Booth Tarkington pictured 'Penrod' as taking umbrage at being called 'a little gentleman.'"

Bragdon took no umbrage and is responsible for passing through his sententious prose most of the direct impressions we have of Ellis. We know from him that Ellis could joke about his poverty: "Art is long and artists are usually short," that he thought pictures should be composed, not copied from nature:

"A man should go sketching with his hands in his pockets." Among other things he thought that "Americans are so fond of nature that they would use the Palisades for advertising purposes and replace the sea beach with ... cement." And, as to his own small following and peculiar reputation, he only commented that "devout Bostonians cross themselves and breathe a prayer when the name of Bulfinch is mentioned, yet if he were among them today they would stone him to death—in the newspapers."

Ellis became a teller of tales illustrated by curious murals and paintings, in which his own earlier architectural achievements are mocked as backgrounds for "fairy stories," of which the "point" might be appreciated only by children.

Ellis, who abandoned architecture (according to his obituary in *The American Architect*) because he was "repelled by the modern practice of the profession," was repelled by much more than that. He was not willing to be one of those—as he described them in an essay on "Puss in Boots"—"who, while feeling their superiority of intelligence, yet bow their heads, forcing themselves to be humble and insinuating." Smug were too many of the people to whom he would have to turn for patronage, and deferential to smugness he could not be.

In the world of triumphant tycoons Harvey Ellis had been an architect of fables—castles for frontier barons and tombs for bishops and heroes. After the depression of 1893 he became the painter of fables. He said "the charm of the fairy tale [lies in] the desire common to all sorts and conditions of men ... to escape from the work-a-day world."

Escape was Ellis's response to a world that was less and less able in years of depression and then less and less willing in years of reaction to accept the fantastic, romantic, or even the innovating spirit in architecture.

In the last two years of his life he worked for Gustave Stickley's *Craftsman* magazine, in Syracuse, designing furniture, textiles, interiors—none of which had the breath of life in them. He was drinking again, in pain, and his story dragged out to a melancholy close. Bragdon, ever attempting to dignify Ellis, suggested how it ended: "He had the dress, bearing, and manners of a gentleman; there was a certain quiet dignity about him, and I think it was never more present, nor better became him, than in that crowded public ward of a city hospital to which (before his friends rallied to his aid) he had been taken, mortally stricken." He died on January 2, 1904.

II

IT WAS NOT UNTIL 1912 that the architectural profession paid much attention to the departure of Harvey Ellis. Then, in a burst of nostalgia, the editors of the *Western Architect* reproduced a series of his designs, small, impractical, painstaking, decorative. It was as if they were commenting ironically both on Ellis's small focus and upon the death that year of Daniel Burnham, who had made famous the expression: "Make no little plans."

Burnham's celebrated phrase was characteristic: "Make no little plans," he had said. "They have no magic to stir men's blood and probably will not be realized. Make big plans; aim high in hope and work, remembering that a noble, logical diagram once recorded will never die, but long after we are gone will be a living thing, asserting itself with ever-growing insistency."

Burnham made it clear that he was not talking of plans for big buildings; in fact, he occasionally let slip the implication that men like Louis Sullivan (and Harvey Ellis perhaps) were impractical, romantic, "paper architects." No, one must aim higher than that: "There are two sorts of architectural beauty; first, that of the individual building; and second, that of an orderly and fitting arrangement of many buildings; the relationship of all the buildings is more important than anything else."

The 1880s and early 1890s had afforded a great opportunity to architects to fashion individual buildings of richness and of fresh design. The next twenty years afforded a larger scope to men as tough, practical, and determined as Daniel Burnham, men with a genius for organization and a capacity to avoid distraction. Those who could deal on equal terms with the magnates of commerce could turn big plans into big realities. Cities could be planned and altered to conform to plan if the planning conformed realistically to increasing real estate values.

Burnham himself contributed mightily to his own opportunities by changing the nature of his own profession and by shrewdly recognizing the rapid changes being worked upon the society around him. To measure his accomplishment, it is necessary to take a broader look at the years after 1880. The settlement and exploitation of the Mississippi Valley presented for the reaping an incredible harvest, a harvest men had not planted. The trees had grown high and thick; the prairie was deep with the accumulated loam of the ages; the prairie animals bore hides which the Indians were prepared to collect in return for a few trinkets and a little bad whiskey. After the harvest of furs came the harvest of lumber and then the harvest of wheat. Riches poured forth from the land almost volcanically. There was hard labor needed to gather up the offerings of the opulent land, but a man with a flair for managing his fellow-men could organize and discipline that labor. Extraction could proceed retarded only by occasional depressions, when the capacity of the earth to pour forth bounty outran the capacity of civilization to absorb it.

In the 1880s a territory larger than that of the thirteen original states was opened to population; or, as Frederick Jackson Turner noted, there was added to the farms of the nation a territory equal to France, Germany, England, and Wales. In Minnesota the population of the six wheat-growing counties in the Red River valley jumped from 21,123 to 71,190 in the decade. St. Paul doubled its population between 1880 and 1883, and doubled it again by 1888, as it profited from its position as a railroad and jobbing center. And no wonder; the lines which it fed were reaching out into the Dakotas, Kansas, and Nebraska while the population of parts of those states quadrupled; railroad mileage in the Dakotas grew from 399 in 1880 to 4,726 in 1890, in Nebraska from 1,634 to 5,407. The Great Northern and the Northern Pacific were pushed through to the West Coast; the range cattle industry moved northward into the trade territory of Minneapolis and St. Paul; and then, accumulating profusion upon profusion, another natural outpouring was added to lumber and burgeoning agriculture; iron ore was found, millions of

Daniel H. Burnham, operator extraordinary, was a different sort of blossom in the flowering of midwestern architecture. He is pictured at the left in a characteristic role—supervising the design for Chicago's Columbian Exposition of 1893, a fair whose architecture bore the marks of Burnham's love for the grandly classical, or, as unadmiring critics Louis Sullivan and Frank Lloyd Wright might have put it, "the dead hand of Rome."

Like most of the truly great buildings designed by the firm of Burnham and Root, Chicago's Rookery was the child of John Wellborn Root. At the right is the outside of the building's spiral staircase. Root died before Burnham's ambitions had reached full flower, and in a night of despair the surviving partner delivered his eulogy: "I have worked, I have schemed and dreamed to make us the greatest architects of the world . . . and now he dies — damn! damn!"

tons of it, on the escarpments of the Lake Superior basin.

In 1884 the first ore was shipped out of Two Harbors from the Vermillion range, bound for Andrew Carnegie's furnaces. James J. Hill and John D. Rockefeller were not long in seizing control of thousands of acres of red oxidized earth, and by 1891 the Messabi range was producing. The population of the lumber and ore port of Duluth leapt from 3,000 in 1880 to 33,000 in 1890. Farther south, Minneapolis used six million board feet of Minnesota lumber to lay sixty-seven miles of boardwalk in a single year (1887).

With the outpouring of natural resources and of wealth in the 1880s came an opportunity for artists, particularly for architects. New cities had to be built to house millions of newcomers, and there was wealth aplenty in the hands of new rich eager to display it. Daniel Burnham sensed an opportunity.

Louis Sullivan and Frank Lloyd Wright sensed it too. Sullivan recalled that when he arrived in the West he "looked at the sky ... raised his hand and cried in full voice: 'This is the place for me!' ... [I] thought it all magnificent and wild, a crude extravaganza, an intoxicating rawness, a sense of big things to be done." Wright, a few years later, felt the intoxication in what he called "that unconsciously – but naturally, thank God! – revolutionary time."

It was a time of wonders. In Chicago Burnham and Root's Monadnock Building and Louis Sullivan's Auditorium Building carried masonry towers higher than they had ever been carried before. In St. Louis the railroad station and Sullivan's Wainwright Building appeared, masterpieces of the first order. In Minneapolis E. Townsend Mix showed in his Metropolitan Building that glass could open out the interiors of office buildings like vertical arcades, and all through the region boldness, ambition, enterprise, and power expressed themselves.

But it was Burnham who best understood a second tendency: that power was flowing into larger and larger combinations. Many years later Louis Sullivan recalled that "during this period there was well underway the formation of mergers, combinations, and trusts in the industrial world. The only architect in Chicago to catch the significance of the movement was Daniel Burnham, for in its tendency toward bigness, organization, delegation, and intense commercialism, he sensed the reciprocal workings of his own mind."

Frank Lloyd Wright, who was less generous in his estimate, called Burnham a "master manager" who "would have been equally great in the hat, cap, or shoe business." But Wright was never one to tolerate rivals, and Burnham was a formidable rival. What had made him so formidable?

He was born in Henderson, New York, in 1846. He moved with his family to Chicago in 1855, graduated from high school there in 1865, but failed to gain entrance to either Harvard or Yale, the goals set for him by ambitious parents (both universities were later to award him honorary degrees). He became a clerk in a retail store but (despite Frank Lloyd Wright) was not a success. Then he became a draftsman in the architectural office of Major Jenney; he had done well in drawing in school. Like Mark Twain, however, he heard the siren song of easy riches in the mines of Nevada and soon departed to seek his fortune there. He failed and returned to Chicago where he tried his hand at politics, running for the state senate. This venture, too, failed, and he formed an architectural partnership. It in turn failed in 1871, and his father took a hand in his career, securing a job for him with the firm of Carter, Drake, and Wight. There, finally, he was fortunate. Among the other young draftsmen in the office was a handsome, articulate, and talented young southerner, John Wellborn Root. With Root's genius for architecture and his own understanding of the practical needs of the profession—case-hardened by failure and with a flair for organization and useful friendships—Burnham's career began a long, unbroken upward path. The volume of work his firm produced increased regularly, and net moved in happy parallel to gross.

The appraisal of Burnham's architectural work is not our concern here but, rather, the understanding of the architect Burnham as a representative frontier figure. Burnham's objectives were early defined, his heroes consciously selected, and his image of himself ever clearer as he grew older and more successful. Harriet Monroe spoke of his "unconquerable egoism"; Sullivan spoke of his "fixed irrevocable purpose" to put himself at the head of the biggest architectural enterprise in the world. This was the ambition, said Sullivan, "for the sake of

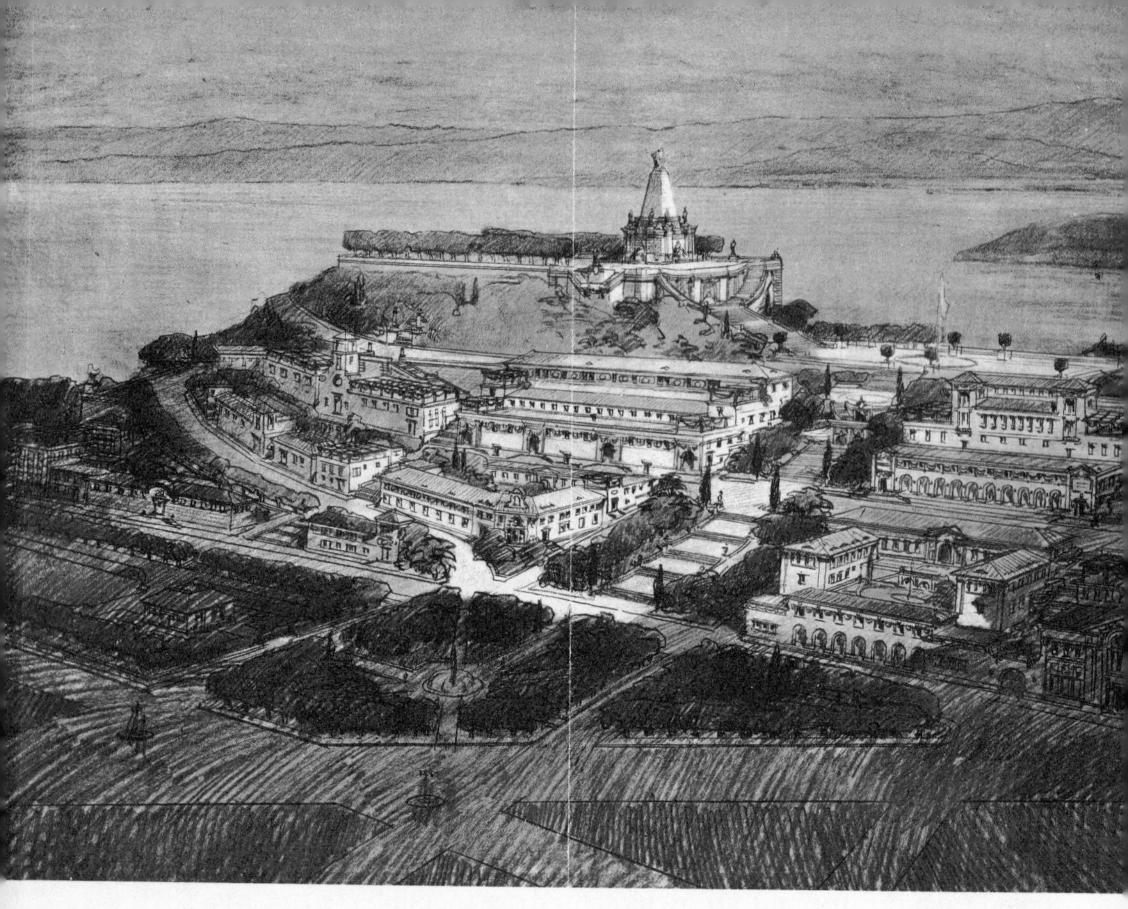

"My idea," Burnham said, "is to work up a big business, to handle big things, deal with big businessmen, and to build up a big organization, for you can't handle big things unless you have an organization." Burnham had acquired his big organization by the turn of the century, and in 1904 the Association for the Improvement and Adornment of San Francisco provided him with the opportunity to handle one of the biggest things imaginable—the redesign of an entire city. Burnham went at it with characteristic sweep, and his Report on a Plan for San Francisco, *published in 1905, was a testament to the scale of his vision:*

"We must remember that a meagre plan will fall short of perfect achievement, while a great one will yield large results, even if it is never fully realized." His plan was not meagre, as the drawings on these pages of Twin Peaks and Telegraph Hill illustrate. The earthquake and fire of 1906 might have given the city the opportunity to implement some of Burnham's ideas, but the need to rebuild quickly argued against the desire to rebuild differently and the "damndest finest ruins" were more or less re-erected: the results can be seen in the photographs of Twin Peaks and Telegraph Hill today.

which he would bend or sacrifice all else." He once told his more artistic colleagues that "my idea is to work up a big business, to handle big things, deal with big businessmen, and to build up a big organization, for you can't handle big things unless you have an organization."

Burnham's organization did handle big things: plans for Manila, Cleveland, Minneapolis, Chicago, and San Francisco. He helped midwesterners understand the beauty of the lakes, the prairie, and the sky; he forced them to make parks of sand-flats and boggy meadows. His was the imagination which rescued the mall between the Washington Monument and the Capitol building from railroad tracks. His mightiest accomplishment was the assemblage of talent which created on Chicago's lakefront the world's Columbian Exposition of 1892-93. His contribution to architecture as an art is a subject of considerable debate. Some critics point out that after Root's death in 1891 D. H. Burnham and Company did good work; Chicago's Reliance Building, in particular, is magnificent. On the other hand, Harriet Monroe, who loved Root and could not bear Burnham's "unconquerable egoism," resented what she said was his claiming credit for the firm's work. Later, Burnham was cast as Lucifer in the cosmic drama written by the admirers of Louis Sullivan, who regarded him as having betrayed western architecture when he turned over control of the Columbian Exposition to eastern practitioners of the "grandiloquent and archaeological" classicist style.

Frank Lloyd Wright called Burnham's influence "a tragic travesty . . . perversion . . . a blight upon our progress . . . a senseless reversion. . . ." Sullivan asserted that it was "the most subtle and slow-acting of poisons . . . an imperceptible miasma within the white shadow of a higher culture . . . the bogus antique . . . snobbish and alien to the land." After Root's death and Sullivan's slow decline from eminence, Burnham's success encouraged allegations (never supported by Sullivan) that he had deliberately isolated Sullivan from his clients by patronizing him as "an impractical artist." By this time, however, it seems likely that Burnham would have sincerely regarded Sullivan as such. He had come to accept completely his role as a thinker of big thoughts, a tycoon among tycoons, moving from commission to commission in his private pullman office.

It had not always been so. His dependence upon Root had been deep and affectionate. He once knew his own limitations, recognizing that he required the artistic stimulus of another. Miss Monroe tells the strange story of Burnham's vigil over the body of his partner. He paced the floor for hours, talking to himself aloud; "he shook his fist and cursed the murderous fates . . . : 'I have worked, I have schemed and dreamed to make us the greatest architects of the world—I have made him see it and kept him at it—and now he dies—damn! damn! damn!'"

There are two aspects of Burnham's character which led him more and more to embrace the classic precedents advocated by the East Coast architects and to abandon the vigorous innovations of his years of partnership with Root. First, he was living in a time when the great tycoons were organizing the reaping of the fruits of the frontier, and these tycoons were popular heroes. Burnham, also, admired the wonderful vigor of the railroad tycoons, the barons of the bonanza farms which stretched across the wheatlands of the Dakotas and the cattle lords of the southwest. Even physical weaklings like E. H. Harriman and Henry Clay Frick had an intensity of purpose which terrified and triumphed. These are the men to whom the frontier yielded its treasures. It is said that when Marshall Field was asked to give information for a genealogical table he replied: "Why do we need a genealogy?" He needed no ghosts to stand behind him; he was clothing a city as Armour was feeding it and Frederick Weyerhaeuser was providing the materials to house it.

Midwesterners were as proud of Marshall Field as he was of himself, but throughout the area the true titans were the railroad builders. Of them it was said by Lord Bryce, Britain's ambassador to the United States, "Railroad kings are among the greatest men, perhaps, I may say, the greatest men, in America. . . . They have power, more power—that is, more opportunity of making their will prevail—than perhaps anyone in political life, except the President and the Speaker, who, after all, hold theirs only for four years and two years, while the railroad monarch may keep his for life."

Louis Sullivan understood Burnham and was fascinated by the growing power of the tycoon image to transform his friend and competitor into a tycoon. Sullivan understood how powerful the chorus was which rang in Burnham's ears:

> All rejoiced ... that these great men, these mighty men, had ... risen from the ranks of the common people ... and their hymn arose and went shimmering as a paean to their mighty ones ... Captains of Industry, Kings of this, Barons of that, Merchant Princes, Railroad Magnates, Wizards of Finance, or, as Burnham said one day to Louis: "Think of a man like Morgan, who can take a man like Cassatt in the palm of his hand and set him on the throne of the Pennsylvania [Railroad]!" And thus, in its way, the populace sang hymns to its heroes.

A second determinant in Burnham's character was his lack of confidence in his own artistic judgment. His agony at the death of Root showed this and so did his prostrating himself before the eastern architects who had had the Beaux Arts training he desperately missed. The famous scene in which he went before the group of easterners assembled to plan the Columbian Exposition was recorded by Sullivan, who served as secretary for the meeting. Burnham began, he wrote, by "progressively and grossly apologizing to the eastern men for the presence of their benighted brethren of the West. Dick Hunt [the venerable Richard Morris Hunt, the first American to graduate from the École des Beaux Arts in Paris, presiding over the gathering] interrupted: 'Hell, we haven't come out here on a missionary expedition. Let's get to work.'" A sense of his cultural inferiority, his lack of an eastern education, dogged Burnham all his life. He was a success: his checkbook made that clear. But was he a great architect?

He was never really sure. He had taken for his hero J. P. Morgan, a poor choice for an artist. In contrast, Louis Sullivan's was Michelangelo, into whose presence he came when, as a student, he visited the Sistine Chapel. Sullivan confronted there "a superman ... a great Free Spirit ... he was filled with the awe that stills. Here he came face to face with the first great adventurer. The first mighty man of courage. The first man with a Great Voice ... the first mighty Craftsman." When Sullivan returned to America, he was determined to demand of himself an achievement as vast as Michelangelo's, to achieve a new archi-

Probably the greatest solid masonry structure of modern times, Chicago's Monadnock Block (center) endures as a monument to John Wellborn Root.

tecture, "to start on the course of practical experimentation ... that no architectural dictum, or tradition, or superstition, or habit should stand in the way."

Burnham made his way to Rome some years later, and his response was somewhat different. His clients were welcoming the classic revival, which he, under the urging of the eastern men, had made the official architecture of the 1893 exposition. They and he had rejected Sullivan's innovations as impractical. Rome was to him not an arena in which Michelangelo struggled to extend the limits of art but a cemetery, where achievement was eternal and unchanging. There he felt that "the fleeting, the transitory, the ephemeral, the self-assertive, the struggle for originality, all seemed to drop out of mind. ..." It was pleasant to have available such a vast inventory of material about which no questions of propriety could be raised and for which there was a steady demand. Pleasant, that is, unless a man were pursuaded he had something better to offer.

However much they may have resented Burnham's egotism and deplored his using the weight of his prestige to advance the classic revival and suffocate the free, experimental architecture of the West, Harriet Monroe, Sullivan, and Wright agreed upon Burnham's good temper and generosity. He was beloved personally. Even Sullivan said he was "open-minded, just, magnanimous." Wright told of an offer by Burnham to send Wright to the École des Beaux Arts, to give the young draftsman the education he had always wanted. But by that time Wright was already a disciple of Sullivan and was hearing voices to which Burnham was deaf. Miss Monroe, trying to be fair, admitted that Burnham had "initiative, strength of will, and a certain splendor of enthusiasm which captured men and held them. ..."

Burnham's generosity and enthusiasm were genuine and were recognized as such by the clients whom he charmed. He shared with them an unquestioning confidence in the world as it was, and he never evidenced any desire to escape from it. His creativity was a practical creativity, and he left his stamp upon great cities. But, somehow, his work is less intriguing, more prosaic than that of Harvey Ellis, whose buildings never quite hold together as compositions because they are always aspiring to be something else. It is a long way from Chicago to Camelot.

Chapter Five

Ignatius Donnelly

Frank Billings Kellogg

I

IGNATIUS DONNELLY DIED OF DERISION. Not his corpulent Red-Irish body, which had survived so many blizzards and dust storms and endless haggling conventions and caucuses—his body died of a heart attack in his sixty-ninth year, two months after he lost his twenty-third election campaign. Nor did his spirit die—it animated the reforms of two Progressive decades built upon his four decades of agitation—and it went marching on into the agriculture policies of the New Deal. But his reputation, that part of his reality which we who seek after him encounter first, was buried under the ridicule of respectable politicians and journalists during his lifetime and respectable historians thereafter. Even during the liberal years, the 1930s and 1940s, Ignatius Donnelly, like William Jennings Bryan, was thought to be too much the hayseed Gracchus, too much the product of the pre-deodorant era, to please the fastidious urban intellectuals.

"Ignominius" Donnelly he was called at the end. He had led the Anti-Monopolists and the Greenbackers and the Grangers and the Populists, had lost so many campaigns for Congress and the Senate and the governorship and the presidency that he had become a figure of fun. William Watts Folwell, the establishment historian of Minnesota, called his life a "dreary record." Latter-day critics agreed. Richard Hofstadter said he had been a leader of "country cranks"; Eric Goldman said he "had a reputation for the kind of theories that too many nights on the prairie can produce."

During Donnelly's lifetime, Folwell set him down as "discredited," a "mountebank politician." He was attacked from the Left: Everett Fish called him a "fat brute," and Sidney Owen called him the "Benedict Arnold of Populism." He was attacked from the Right: the St. Paul *Pioneer Press* said he was "like Judas Iscariot," "a dictator" and "a dog"; the *Mississippi Valley Lumberman* called him a "dishonest political juggler," and during a famous exchange of invective, the stately Elihu Washburne of Illinois accused him of taking bribes, of being an "office beggar," a coward, a liar and a criminal "whose record is stained with every fraud . . . a man who has proved false alike to his friends, his constituents, his country, his religion, and his God."

Donnelly was quite capable of sustaining this sort of discourse. He replied to Washburne seriatim, pausing upon the matter of office-begging to note that four Washburne brothers had sat in the House of Representatives (Folwell piously notes "with honorable records") and that "out of office they are miserable, wretched . . . as the famous stump-tailed bull in fly time . . . every young male of the gentleman's family is born into the world with 'M. C.' [Member of Congress] franked across his broadest part. The great calamity seems to be that God, in his infinite wisdom, did not make any of them broad enough for the letters 'U. S. S.' [U.S. Senate]." Donnelly gave his valedictory to Washburne in these words:

> And if there be in our midst one low sordid, vulgar soul; one barren, mediocre intelligence; one heart callous to every sentiment and every generous impulse, one tongue leprous with slander; one mouth which like unto a den of the foul beast giving forth deadly odors; if there be one character which, while blotched and spotted all over, yet raves and rants and blackguards like a prostitute; if there be here one bold, bad, empty, bellowing demagogue, it is the gentleman from Illinois.

Ignatius Donnelly, the pugnacious Irish politician-speculator-farmer-writer-philosopher who took his resemblance to Stephen A. Douglas seriously.

Though Donnelly's words were thought to have been so intemperate as to cast him beyond the pale of parliamentary discourse, Washburne's did not cost him *his* power and place. Why the difference? Their language was equally sulfurous. But Washburne was, according to Folwell, "distinguished"; he was rich and related to other rich and distinguished men. Much could be forgiven him. Donnelly was poor and Irish, and he did not acknowledge any man to be his better. A friend, Major Thomas Newson, reviewing Donnelly's career, concluded:

> Had his sense of propriety or even policy enabled him to have endured the slings of his enemies quietly . . . it is possible he would have saved himself the opposition he has since encountered, but that would not have been Donnelly. . . . he resented what he felt was a wrong. . . . The combative elements of the man have kept him in political hot water for nearly twenty years.

Newson was writing in 1884. Actually the water had been hot for thirty years and remained at a slow boil for sixteen more. Another friend, Wilford L. Wilson, said that Donnelly had "fallen in the esteem of the cultivated, refined, and religious people who largely make up the Republican party," while Washburne and his brothers went on to greater eminence among these same people. Folwell said that if Donnelly had spared that final excoriation of Washburne, "his own future and that of Minnesota politics would have been different from the dreary record."

What was that record? Was it really so dreary? Now that the tempers of a vehement generation have cooled, can the man, Ignatius Donnelly, be described without patronage or billingsgate?

Ignatius Donnelly was never a part of any community in which his status was secure, in which peers steadily exchanged esteem and reassurance. If that is an "establishment," it was never open to him. From the outset he was an outsider. His father was an anticlerical Irish immigrant who had barely begun the practice of medicine in Philadelphia when he contracted typhus from a patient and died. The education of the children, like the medical schooling of the father, was financed by the pawnshop kept by the proud, stiff, domineering mother.

The city was aglow at night, but not with brotherly love. Long afterward Donnelly recalled that "Philadelphia was afflicted by many riots; riots between whites and blacks, between natives and foreigners, between the different churches and different fire companies." Especially after the panic of 1837 there were riots with the "Native Americans," "Know-Nothings," who feared competition for jobs from the Irish newcomers. The Irish were accustomed to civil disorder. They had a long inheritance of suspicion and resentment of authority. And the "Native Americans" resented the Irish. "If an Irishman is hanged for murder, his nativity is freely admitted," Donnelly commented, "but if he distinguishes himself in an honorable walk of life, then it is discovered that he is Scotch-Irish."

Ignatius Donnelly was proud of his heritage, although the signs "Dogs and Irish, Keep Out" were constant reminders of a bitter welcome and although, as a non-Catholic who attended public schools, he was not a member of the "club of the Irish" either. After he had written *The Great Cryptogram*, a half century later, he remembered his pride in his father's love of literature and his own encouragement by the great Oliver Wendell Holmes (to whom he had sent a youthful poem). "A good many people believe that the proper occupation for a person of Irish blood in digging a ditch or flourishing a shillelagh. They are presumed to know nothing about literature and ultimately lack those qualities of patience and perseverance which are held to be the birthright of the Anglo-Saxon.... I think I have done something to dispel that prejudice."

After high school he studied law in the aristocratic ménage of Benjamin Harris Brewster, who was to become the attorney general of Pennsylvania and later of the United States. Brewster and his clerks were courteous, correct, but distant. "I lived with them, as it were, *per gratia.* The bond of connection has never been a pleasant one—I sever it without regret," he said after three years. Then Donnelly began his political career as he would end it, indifferent to party but vehement in his identification with the underdog. His maiden speech was for the Democrats in Independence Square, supporting an open immigration policy. He ran for the state legislature but finally supported the Whig candidate, who took a strong anti-Know-Nothing position.

In June of 1856 he was back with the Democrats, attacking the Republicans and their Know-Nothing allies as "holding midnight council over the Irish and the Dutchman."

Two years earlier he had married Kate McCaffrey, the daughter of a shopowner, after a family dispute. It was, he later recalled, "the most ludicrous affair imaginable ... the pawnshop broker's shop and the market stall holding a heraldic disputation." His stern, ambitious mother resisted the match, and he resisted her, finally deciding in 1856 to make a new start in the West. She never forgave Kate, although she did admit in later years that Ignatius could not have prospered so well in Philadelphia as, for a while, he did in Minnesota.

The young Irishman went west on the make. He told a high school friend that "money makes the man, the want of it the fellow." He had seen enough of poverty. "Seneca praised the beauties of poverty, but Seneca had a large income. The beauties of poverty! It is nothing but unsatisfied wants, restricted capabilities, undeveloped virtues...." His ancestors and his brothers had had enough of that! One way to wealth was through real estate speculation. As a young lawyer in Philadelphia he had learned about land promotion, serving as an officer of five emigrant aid associations. He toured the new states of the Northwest and settled on Minnesota as the place to make his fortune: "What a beautiful land has the red man lost and the white man won!"

Despite his awareness of its beauty, Donnelly was not sentimental about the West in its primitive state. He had read Cooper, but to him land was real estate. His was a dream of golden prairies producing a crop of dollar bills as settlers came upon them ready to pay the man well who had gotten there first. Donnelly saw the peaceful land "waiting for the crowding numbers and the clamorous competition of the human animal to flow in...." He arrived during the great land rush of the 1850s. Emigration spilled out upon the land. In six years 140,000 people came flooding in where only 4,000 had been. A St. Paul newspaper admitted that "a very subordinate attention was paid to farming, the interest of the community being principally absorbed in projects of speculation." Major Newson said: "Almost everybody went into the business of buying and selling real estate, procuring acres and laying them out into cities and selling corner lots at fabulous prices. It became a mania."

Donnelly went into partnership with John Nininger, brother-in-law of the powerful Alexander Ramsey, territorial governor of Minnesota. Together they bought one thousand or more acres along the Mississippi fifteen miles southeast of St. Paul, attracted investors, and became "land sharks." On the emigrant packet boats "Bill Mallen . . . with his marked cards, and Ingeneous Doemly [*sic*], with his city lots on paper selling for a thousand dollars each" were equal hazards.

But Donnelly believed his own propaganda. Mortgage debt in the territory grew from $22,553 in 1853 to $2,124,071 in 1854, and he borrowed with the rest to improve his cloud city. Among a hundred houses built on the vast plat, he commenced a mansion for himself; in his fever he thought himself a millionaire. After all, tax valuations in Minnesota had grown from $3,500,000 in 1854 to nearly $50,000,000 in 1857. Everybody was getting rich.

Then the bubble broke. In the summer of 1857 the credit system of the West collapsed. It was said that half the population of St. Paul retreated to the East. Hundred of townsites returned to weeds, and Donnelly, in September of that bleak year, failed to pay his creditors. The collapse of 1857 had three crucial consequences for him: it drove him back from prosperity, back into the arms of the debtors and the poor; it drove him into farming, (for he had to do something with land which would never, now, contain a city); and it drove him back into full-time politics.

Donnelly, the disappointed land shark struggling to pay his own debts, refused to join in Nininger's squeezing of payments from those on his townsite who could not produce the full price asked before the collapse of the land boom. He was no more disposed toward idealism than before. "Self-defense is the first instinct of nature and the first duty to ourselves. A man who would take the clothes off his back to give his creditors would only be kicked for his pains." The partnership broke up, and Donnelly gained the friendship of his neighbors and an increasing solidarity with the debtor class. At the same time, he was still dependent upon the patronage of Alexander Ramsey, who supplied him with legal work and political opportunity. It was

A Mississippi Valley farm. It was on such land as this that Donnelly had hoped to build a new Eden and in the process build himself a fortune. Both dreams withered, done in by circumstance and the vagaries of speculation. If it gave him nothing else, however, the experience gave him an understanding of the hardship of the farmer's life that would help shape the course of his political life.

a convenience that his long-standing aversion to slavery coincided with Ramsey's patronage, for in the pre–Civil War years he became an organization Republican. After two unsuccessful races for the state senate, he became Ramsey's hand-picked lieutenant governor in 1859. He was off to a good start and persisted as a Janissary of the Ramsey dynasty for nearly a decade. He shifted to the U.S. Congress in 1862 at the urging of his wife ("Money to live on and glory to die on," she said), his creditors ("If I am [elected] I will be able to do something for you," he said to them), and Ramsey. His three terms in Congress were the lowest period (morally—not in terms of "success" or the opinion of his contemporaries) of his political life. They manifested the moral, political, and economic depravity of wartime and Reconstruction. Donnelly was, except on rare occasions, a typical Ramsey Radical Republican, covering railroad lobbying and personal speculation with empty patriotic forensics.

In 1864 he sold to speculators information about government commodities dealings, and he took railroad stock in exchange for supporting land grants. In 1867 he took more stock for delaying the passage of a land grant until promotors could buy ripe townsites. In 1869 he was involved with General John C. Frémont in fraud and bankruptcy in the promotion of the Atlantic and Pacific Railroad. Throughout the period he was one of Jay Cooke's chief congressional agents.

All the time, however, the instincts of the outsider were growing stronger. He differed with Ramsey and the "dynasty" over the tariff issue, believing that high tariffs were penalizing consumers. The bitterness which burst out in his reply to Washburne indicates that he felt himself increasingly isolated from the millers, lumbermen, and railroad builders who were Washburne's "Anglo-Saxon" friends. Through the St. Paul *Globe*, he spoke of the "cold-blooded, purse-proud aristocracy characteristic of Washburne," and he finally broke openly with Ramsey's machine in both the congressional and the Senate campaigns of 1868. He still lobbied for Cooke, but in 1870 when he ran for Congress, supported by the Democrats and the Peoples Party, he lost again as Cooke's contractors organized against him.

Donnelly was still not ready to make a complete break. Though he told a crowd that "railroads . . . were created to transport the commerce of the country, not to rule its politics or corrupt its laws," he succumbed to the blandishing agents of Ramsey and returned to the Republican fold "like a drowned gopher." He had committed no sin in his flirtation with the Democrats, he told a convention, for, like a boy caught fishing on the Sabbath, he said, "I hain't ketched nuthin."

His reconciliation was deceptive. Ramsey's intermediaries feared Donnelly's nature, which one of them called "sanguine . . . pugnacious," and they were right. Donnelly was moving to the left, impelled by character and by his experience on the farming frontier to assume more and more the role of the paladin of the downtrodden farmer, a role which, despite many changes of his party uniform, he never abandoned for the rest of his life.

Consider the strange, halting, anguished progress of Ignatius Donnelly's romance with the farmer. He was a son of the city, no lover of the open country, a rustic in spite of himself. He found himself forced to find another use for land that had been intended for a town. Only then did he resort to farming. Even after he had tried to supervise his tenants at Nininger (named for his friend) and had started an agricultural society, his speeches were still those of a physiocrat rather than a sodbuster. Anyone else would have been laughed off the podium; he was eloquent enough to be taken seriously when he advised his listeners, in 1860, to set aside an acre as "Mind's Acre" for the cultivation of the intellect.

In 1864 Donnelly was still using the rhythms of his Philadelphia speeches, invoking the image of a golden bridge between the hungry masses of Europe and "a billion empty acres" on this side of the Atlantic. He was for filling those acres with farmers, but he had few of the agrarian illusions of the eighteenth century or of contemporary romantics. Natty Bumppo had never persuaded him of the virtue of Indian conditions, and the condition of frontier farmers he knew to be little better. Dumping millions of unprepared townsmen upon the land would not make them into free and independent yeomen, no matter how many congressional incantations were made over their heads. Idealism without aid in the form of tools and money and education did not impress him. "A human being on 80 acres of unimproved land is as helpless as if he were on 80 acres of water—in fact more so, for he could get a fishing line and probably catch something to eat." Land was a commodity like any other. "Hang on to your land to the last gasp," he told the farmers; "there are no more Minnesotas on the planet; and every day the battle of life will grow fiercer."

The real Ignatius Donnelly, city-bred and reluctant farmer, is an inconvenience to those who would employ him as a stock figure of the rustic romantic. Literary historians like Larzer Ziff who write with clarity and compassion about urban social critics are made uncomfortable by Donnelly's apocalyptic novel *Caesar's Column*, written during a period of despair when he feared that the just resentments of the farmers and workers would find no redress from the plutocracy. Ziff winces at what he calls "the familiar high-flown changes on biblical rhetoric . . . the romantic lyrics of the cardboard motto, written to be sung to the accompaniment of the melodeon" of Donnelly's preamble to the Populist platform of 1892. Literary commentators, more fastidious than compassionate, have often pictured Donnelly falsely, underrating his capacity to appraise the reality of American life, and, therefore, they perpetuate the myth that he was ineffectual.

Ziff deprecates Donnelly as "romantic in a relatively unconscious fashion," unable to take a roundhouse swing at social problems because reality was for him "cushioned." His imagination, it seems, "still lingered in an Eden of sentimental patriotism." He and the rest of rural America were "naïve and sullenly defensive," believing that if foreign conspiracies would pass away, there would be "an Eden regained." It might be well at this point to take a look at the Eden which Donnelly himself knew on the farm and what he said about it. Was he a bumpkin ignoramus? Had he no specific measures to improve the farmer's condition, and had he no success in bringing these measures into law?

The 1870s were a gloomy period in his political career. He had been reduced "to his fists and his backbone." He borrowed money and took his sons to farm an unbroken prairie in Stevens County, where there was no glade, no sheltering oak or pine to

EMIGRATION

UP THE MISSISSIPPI RIVER.

The attention of Emigrants and the Public generally, is called to the now rapidly improving

TERRITORY OF MINNESOTA,

Containing a population of 150,000, and goes into the Union as a State during the present year. According to an act of Congress passed last February, the State is munificently endowed with Lands for Public Schools and State Universities, also granting five per cent. on all sales of U. S. Lands for Internal Improvements. On the 3d March, 1857, grants of Land from Congress was made to the leading Trunk Railroads in Minnesota, so that in a short time the trip from New Orleans to any part of the State will be made in from two and a half to three days. The

CITY OF NININGER,

Situated on the Mississippi River, 35 miles below St. Paul, is now a prominent point for a large Commercial Town, being backed by an extensive Agricultural, Grazing and Farming Country; has fine streams in the interior, well adapted for Milling in all its branches; and Manufacturing **WATER POWER** to any extent.

Mr. JOHN NININGER, (a Gentleman of large means, ideas and liberality, speaking the various languages,) is the principal Proprietor of **Nininger**. He laid it out on such principles as to encourage all **MECHANICS**, Merchants, or Professions of all kinds, on the same equality and footing; the consequence is, the place has gone ahead with such rapidity that it is now an established City, and will annually double in population for years to come.

Persons arriving by Ship or otherwise, can be transferred without expense to Steamers going to Saint Louis; or stop at Cairo, and take Railroad to Dunleith (on the Mississippi). Steamboats leave Saint Louis and Dunleith daily for **NININGER**, and make the trip from Dunleith in 36 to 48 hours.

Nininger City was Donnelly's abortive thrust into the financial big time—and a failure that bankrupted his pocket, if not quite his spirit.

break the wind sweeping down from the Arctic. The land cost one dollar an acre, but three times as much was required to turn the sod with a steel plow. His recourse to full-time farming opened him to the ridicule of his urban enemies. They enjoyed the spectacle of Donnelly working his land. Said the St. Paul *Pioneer Press*: "Woe to the usurer, the wheat-scalper, or the grasshopper that tries to pitch his tent therein." Grasshoppers were no joke to the farmer that year. The Rocky Mountain locust fell upon Stevens County. In the towns "the very lawns [were] eaten bare by them"; the wheatfields were ravaged. Farmers desperately tried to drive them off by dragging ropes or to destroy them with coal tar and sheet-iron scoops.

Remembering those days, Kate Donnelly wrote her husband, "When I think of farming—I get almost sick. Think how hard they work—and they invariably come out in debt—and then [more] borrowing... and then misery—life is scarcely worth having."

It was no romantic dream of an American Eden that distracted Donnelly from accomplishing specific reforms. It was the disorganization of most city workers, who had not yet learned to share in an effective coalition with the farmers (the Populist campaigns were lost in the cities), and the well-financed and cleverly directed political resistance to reform. He knew precisely who benefited from the pricing policies, monetary policies, and excessive economic power from which the farmer suffered: those who sold supplies and lent money to farmers and those who bought his produce and carried it to market. Ziff, apparently basing his estimate on one of Donnelly's many books and a few paragraphs from the preamble to a party platform, concludes that Donnelly was guilty not only of old-fashioned rhetoric but of a lack of appreciation for wealth, art, sex, and literacy.

Was he so benighted? We have seen that he coveted wealth and despised poverty, that he aspired to literary achievement. Despite Ziff's prejudices, Donnelly did not represent "the morality of a rural upbringing," nor were his "principles instilled on the farm." But granting Ziff a little license, was Donnelly guilty of the illusion that there was a nasty "connection between riches, art, and sexuality"? Was the "midwestern imagination" the pathetic shriveled blossom "of a culture in which learning was embellishment and counterspell rather than criticism and liberation"? Did he behave as if he felt that "the artifacts of civilization, unknown on the farm, were equated with viciousness"? Whose farm? Not Ignatius Donnelly's farm. It might be fair to wonder whose library is so large, broad, and deep as was Donnelly's. Donnelly was a man of letters, who drew upon his reading to write very well indeed—better than most of his critics.

Like his father, he was widely acquainted with the literature of the Elizabethan period. Out of this reading, not out of "too many lonely nights on the prairie," came his enormous volumes about that period, asserting that Francis Bacon, and not Shakespeare, was the author of the plays and sonnets. No critic has alleged with any success that Donnelly's effort came out of superficial knowledge of the time. William Ewert Gladstone and many others wrote Donnelly to commend him on *The Great Cryptogram*, and there are some who are still persuaded that Donnelly was right. Out of his admiration of Bacon's *New Atlantis* probably arose his own *Atlantis,* requiring researches in the Platonic literature, in Greek and Roman myth, and his groping toward a sort of pioneering comparative anthropology. He did not produce *The Golden Bough,* but he was writing in the 1880s, and he did produce *Dr. Huquet and the Golden Bottle,* which was a remarkable work of the imagination, in some ways antedating William Styron's *Confessions of Nat Turner.* And his exercise in astronomy and geology *Ragnarok* is a fascinating failure.

This is not the place to attempt a complete reappraisal of Donnelly as a man of letters (which is, of course, as worthy a title for him as it was for a much less imaginative novelist like Disraeli). Our primary concern is the history of Donnelly as a political realist, well acquainted with the needs of the farmer and seeking remedies in wide research and a strong and frequently successful political base. Since it was not in their interest to agree with his prescription, his detractors attempted to discredit his diagnosis and his motives for making it. Both that motivation and the validity of that diagnosis should be examined afresh.

Even in his days as a landshark, lobbyist, and spoilsman, he was redeemed by his generous spirit. He still recalled how it was to be "poor and powerless" in Philadelphia and extended his sympathies and energies to aid Negroes and Indians. An Irishman could remember "the people of my blood, my ancestors, [who] for generations led lives of savages and peasants, in mud hovels, without comfort, pleasure, or enlightenment." While antipathy to slavery might have been expected from a northwestern Republican, Donnelly went beyond the convenient conventions of his place and time. He knew education and job opportunity were necessary to the advancement of all distressed minorities, and he espoused these for the Negro and, remarkably for his time, for the Indian.

His courageous insistence upon justice for Indians put him in conflict not only with Ramsey's Republicans but also with Henry M. Rice's Democratic ring. Donnelly, in the Congress during the Sioux outbreak of 1862–63, unflinchingly adopted the unpopular views of Sibley and Joseph R. Brown while his constituents were howling for more dead Indians and for the political scalps of "Indian lovers."

A year after "the outbreak" Donnelly ripped into the Indian agents' exploitation of the Chippewa, though those agents included former Senator Rice (who dominated St. Paul's politics) and friends of the unimpeachable John S. Pillsbury, probably the most powerful citizen of Minneapolis. Donnelly's persistence in espousing a humane Indian policy has been dismissed by some recent critics as utopian, but it won the praise of old Joseph R. Brown, who reviewed it carefully and said "it breathes the true spirit of Indian improvement." Brown, Sibley, and Jonathan Fletcher knew the Indians well, and the endorsement of Brown carries weight.

Donnelly cannot be set down as a dreamer of impractical dreams. Despite Eric Goldman's peculiar assertion, Nininger was a townsite promotion, not "a community where everybody was to love everybody else." Donnelly, the speculator, learned the woes of single-crop farming in the 1850s and 1860s. In 1873 the experience was repeated; another panic deposited upon humble folk the debris of speculators' overreaching. Like the collapse of 1857, the panic of 1873 spread because of the failure of credit, possibly from tight money policies. In this case, the bubble had been blown by Donnelly's old patron, Jay Cooke. Cooke's failure had its most dramatic effects upon Duluth, the town which he, with Donnelly's aid, had "boomed" where the Northern Pacific Railroad touched Lake Superior. After Cooke's fall, half the businesses in the city went bankrupt within sixty days; thousands went hungry and cold; the population dwindled from 5,000 to 1,300; the driver of the town's fire engine quit because there were no funds to fuel it, and in 1877 the city government simply resigned its charter.

It was not strange that many midwesterners thought eastern financial manipulators had undue influence upon the life of the region. Jay Cooke's fortunes recovered, but it took the development of the iron range to bring Duluth back to life. Panics and booms were dramatic, but it was the drab daily evidence of concentrated power which slowly drove Donnelly into open opposition to the railroads. Rates were rigged so that it took half the value of a shipment of wheat to convey it to the Chicago market. Systems were built with bonds, and then stock was floated for a promoter's profit "to go home with."

Jay Gould, Jim Fiske, William Vanderbilt, E. H. Harriman bought and sold the transportation systems upon which the agricultural west depended; they encouraged the settlement of desert regions with false promises and then sought to repay their bondholders with the proceeds of excessive rates. They bought and sold legislators (as Donnelly knew first hand) and judges, too. They built palaces (some of them designed by Harvey Ellis and John Root and Daniel Burnham) while country people drank dust and sank under a burden of malnutrition, overwork, and debt.

Donnelly attacked the midwesterners' grievances with a series of specific remedies, and he was often successful. As early as 1871 he pursuaded the Republicans to adopt a platform calling for a graduated income tax to lighten the property tax load on the farmers. Through Donnelly's exertions his debtor constituents received protection against usurious interest rates and quick foreclosures of their farm machinery. Their children were given fair prices on schoolbooks because of his textbook law and his exposure of the publishers' ring. Many of his proposals during the Granger period ultimately became law, including a

The monetary theories of the "greenbackers" met with stiff derision in the public press, as with this "money-scarecrow" cartoon in Frank Leslie's.

commission to regulate the rates charged by railroads, and his persistent efforts to secure electoral reforms during the Populist period gave greater protection to "plain people" against the machines and corporate control of state legislatures.

The deprecatory opinions of later critics seeking to persuade us that Donnelly was an inept windbag do not agree with the howls of his bruised opponents who had to gather themselves up out of the dust after many a legislative session. Said the St. Paul *Daily Press:* Donnelly "rules the Senate with lawless license of demagogic deviltry, as the commune ruled Paris." In 1887, well after his prime, he introduced fifty-seven measures into the Minnesota legislature, eighteen of which were accepted, either entirely or in amended form.

The effort of the *Daily Press* to paint Donnelly with red was to be expected, but the facts are that in the years of violence in the West, when grievances exploded in terrorism and there were pitched battles between strikers and militia, Donnelly consistently opposed violence. This was true in 1877 and again in 1894. Skillfully and consistently, he sought legislative remedies. After the Granger movement died like a tired warhorse beneath him, he went slogging along ahead of the threadbare Farmers Alliance, still having the respect of the Republicans. Russell Nye to the contrary, Donnelly did not "climb aboard" the Alliance bandwagon. It was a haywagon, and he pulled it. Even the hostile Folwell had to admit how significant was his espousal of its program. "The Republican convention listened to the overture and to Donnelly's delicious blarney and straightway lifted into their platform substantially all the 'demands' of the Alliance and its associates."

Donnelly's objectives were frequently achieved by forcing governors and senators into timely acquiescence. He had encouraged the entrance into politics of Cushman K. Davis, who became governor and then senator by adopting reforms at a prudent distance in time from Donnelly's espousal, as did others such as John Lind, Knute Nelson, and Frank B. Kellogg. In the 1890s, while he was running for governor and vice-president, and seeking the Populist nomination for president, he was still active as a state legislator, with more achievements to his credit. Martin Ridge has pointed out how frequently those who were most vociferous in their public excoriation of him sought his private counsel on specific legislative problems.

Donnelly was also a highly successful investigator. In the decade following his Indian Bureau exposures of the 1860s, he demonstrated the overcharges made on books for the school system and the depredations of the lumbermen upon state lands. For this, of course, he was not beloved by the publishers' or timbermen's lobbies. Folwell, friend of the lumbermen, charged that Donnelly's investigations were "leading nowhere," but they led in the 1880s to the exposure of the iron ore frauds of some of Folwell's friends. In the 1890s Donnelly investigated a monopoly guilty of fixing prices on hard coal and lumbermen guilty of tax evasion. Folwell excised from his *History* the names of most of the plunderers because "by making liberal benefactions to churches, communities, and colleges [they] have brought forth fruit meet for repentance."

Most scholars agree now that Donnelly wrote the most pungent documents of the Populist revolt. He animated the councils of that party, and his oratory could still rouse a crowd. Though John Hicks, Populism's historian, scored him for "florid rhetoric," Donnelly's words forced understanding: the abuses against which they were directed would not have yielded to sweet diffidence. The call for initiative, referendum, and direct primaries was heeded, and Hicks himself sums up the era with the statement that Theodore Roosevelt's presidential messages "read like the preamble to the Populist platform"—written by Ignatius Donnelly fifteen years earlier.

The contribution made by hot Populism to cool Progressivism is now established, even among those who persist in treating Ignatius Donnelly as a joke. But what of his radical views on the money question? It is for their views on the money question that he, and the Greenbackers, Alliancemen, and Populists he led have been most severely derided. Just how silly were his monetary views? Was he a realist, laboring to meet his constituents' needs in practical ways, or was he a crank? Upon the answer to these questions must rest the reputation of Ignatius Donnelly.

As the computers spew forth data for a new generation of economists, Donnelly's views are becoming more sensible. He saw a slowly growing money supply as the cause of a long defla-

"Society divides itself into two hostile camps," Donnelly had written in Ceasar's Column. *In 1877, the hostile camps of labor and capital clashed in a great railroad strike (from* Frank Leslie's Illustrated Newspaper, *August 11, 1877).*

tion, which persisted during the thirty years after the Civil War and which wrought hardship upon the midwestern farmer. He refused to be intimidated by the learned and respectable opinion of the economists of the 1880s about the gold standard; with characteristic independence of mind he saw the matter much as do many learned and respectable economists of the 1960s. He called the gold standard a "relic of barbarism"; Walter Heller (President Kennedy's chief economic adviser) recently called gold "a barbarous metal." Donnelly called for the abolition of a gold standard and the substitution of "fiat money" like the Greenbacks of the Civil War period, and so does Milton Friedman, who was Barry Goldwater's chief economic adviser—or, at least, his most respected source of economic advice. Donnelly, though preferring abolition of "metalism," would settle for a silver standard as a way of producing a more abundant currency and avoiding violent gold-associated international panics. Friedman, reviewing the silver controversy, has stated:

> on the whole the adoption of silver would have been preferable [to a commitment to gold]. . . . Adoption of silver by the United States would certainly have moderated or eliminated deflationary tendencies here. It would also have moderated and might have eliminated deflation in the world at large. . . . If one regards the deflationary price trend as an evil and a horizontal price trend as preferable, as we do, though with some doubts, silver would on this account and for that period have been preferable to gold.

The long deflation from 1865 to 1893 penalized the debtor class and favored creditors. A midwestern farmer who borrowed "100-cent dollars" in 1870 was forced to repay in dollars worth 150 cents, 200 cents, or, if his note could be imagined to come due as late as 1890, even 300 cents. Ignatius Donnelly foresaw this and protested against national monetary policies which artifically increased the value of the dollar. The picture before him, seen in detail, was this: Throughout the post–Civil War period western farmers were heavy borrowers. In 1890, for example, the census showed that, though it was a relatively poor state, Kansas had the highest ratio of mortgage debt to true value of taxed real estate of any state except prosperous New

York. Nebraska, the Dakotas, and Minnesota were all within the top nine states in these ratios. In Kansas and North Dakota there was a mortgage for every two people, and in South Dakota, Nebraska, and Minnesota there was one to every three. In many wheat counties total mortgage debt was close to three-quarters of true valuation.

During the same period the dollar was appreciating in value against a cost index largely made up of farm products. Alex M. Arnett has shown that if the dollar's "commodity value" were set at a base of 100 in 1865, it reached 200 in 1876, 250 in 1885, and 300 in 1894. Milton Friedman surveyed the period from 1867 to 1960 and concluded that deflation was so severe in the post–Civil War decade that "in no other period did wholesale prices fall so continuously at so high a rate" and that "prices fell at a rate of over 1 percent a year from 1879 to 1897." The farmer felt the consequences in two ways. The weight of his debts doubled and redoubled, and the value of his crop shriveled.* During the same period, naturally enough, it took fewer and fewer dollars to buy wheat or corn; as a result, the farmer's return for his labor diminished.**

Recent scholarship has indicated that this long deflation occurred in large measure because the national government, largely in the hands of creditors and heavily influenced by international financiers, wanted it that way.

In 1865 Treasury Secretary McCullogh deliberately set in motion a return to "constitutional currency," meaning a gold standard. The farming West had expanded rapidly to meet the needs of wartime, had borrowed Greenbacks to do so, and McCullogh was using pious words to espouse a tax upon debtors. The government had issued paper money, not redeemable in gold, and the chief business of the states east of the Rockies was being done in such currency. McCullogh's "return" meant that he and his financial friends were determined to force repay-

*Arnett suggests that, because of deflation, the burden of a five-year debt grew during the period when most of the agricultural Northwest was being settled and debt incurred: 1865-69 by 35 percent, 1870-74 by 19.7 percent, 1875-79 by 4.5 percent, 1888-90 by more than 11 percent.

**Wheat prices wobbled downward from 106.7 cents on December 1 for the years 1870-73 to 100.6 cents for 1878-81, 80.2 cents for 1882-85, 74.8 cents for 1886-89, 70.9 cents for 1890-93, and 63.3 cents for 1894-97. Prices as low as 45 cents a bushel were not unknown.

ment in gold by depreciating the currency. Friedman and Anna J. Schwartz have demonstrated that the money stock fell "precipitously" from 1867 to 1879; not until the 1931-39 period "was there anything like it." Then, after a "deflation of 50 percent [which] took place over the course of the decade and a half after 1865," leaders of the farmers, like Donnelly, abandoned their wary view of deflation (Donnelly had been for a mild, slow return to prewar prices) and came out fighting.

Talk of "constitutional currency" did not impress them. They found no ukase for deflation in the Constitution. Donnelly wanted no more pieties about that document; he wanted debts to be repaid in the same currency that had been obtained from the lender. "Can you keep a room warm next winter, with the thermometer at 30 below zero, by reciting the Declaration of Independence?" he asked.

Scholars are in dispute about the diagnosis of this price decline. Friedman and Anna Schwartz have written that "contemporary discussion . . . attributed falling prices and depressed conditions largely to the behavior of the stock of money—and rightly so in the sense that, given a rapid rate of economic growth, the price decline would have been avoided only by a more rapid rise in the stock of money." Richard Hofstadter (in his introduction to *Coin's Financial School*) does not take Greenbacker and Populist monetary arguments too seriously and attributes much of the decline to diminished foreign consumption of American farm products. It is difficult for laymen to arbitrate the controversy; the landscape is a bog of statistical quicksand. Our purpose here is merely to indicate that Donnelly, whose contemporary discussion was very audible, was speaking sensibly and might have been right.

The stock of money was subject to Treasury Department influence. Paul M. O'Leary has recently suggested that Donnelly and others were right in seeing a "goldbug" plot behind the deflationary legislation of 1873. President Grant pressed the deflation downward when, under the influence of creditors, he vetoed an act to continue the issuance of a limited supply of irredeemable currency. The farmer paid the price for a national policy of shrinking the money supply.

Friedman analyzed the consequences: "An unusually rapid

rise in output converted an unusually slow rate of rise in the stock of money into a rapid decline in prices." In 1887 an unsophisticated farm journalist put the effect of this decline in simple terms: "There is something wrong in our . . . system. The railroads have never been so prosperous, and yet agriculture languishes. The banks have never done better . . . and yet agriculture languishes. Manufacturing enterprises never made more money . . . and yet agriculture languishes. Towns and cities flourish and 'boom' . . . and yet agriculture languishes."

The farmer had gone west pursuaded of his special virtues. The national romance taught by Thomas Jefferson had schooled him so. By the 1890s he had been pursuaded by deflation and by adversity of his special tribulation. He rose up in the Greenback and Granger and Populist movements and, inarticulate, he sought a voice. For forty years, the great parties vacillated between the requirements of silver lobbyists and gold lobbyists, but there were many who did not comprehend and many who did not care. Ignatius Donnelly gave the farmer a voice. He often spoke too loud, but more often than not he was right in what he said.

It was the supply of money which interested the farmer. He lost the fight, by Grant's veto, to keep the Greenbacks in circulation, and he slowly lost the purchasing power of his crops as farm prices declined and the cost of credit increased.

Unfortunately the supply-of-money issue became confused with the sideshow over free silver. "Bimetalism" was distracting, and ultimately fatal, to the farmer's fight for a growing, noncontracting money supply. Donnelly always saw it so and resisted to the end the reduction of the reformer's platform from a dozen or more specific measures to the narrow question of the free coinage of silver. But the financial pressure of the silver magnates and the urge of politics toward simplification were too great for him, and when in the 1890s, gold suddenly became cheaper, the whole effort to assure a congruence of economic growth with growth in the currency supply was put to sleep by the formal return to the gold standard in 1900. Fresh discoveries of gold in South Africa, Colorado, and the Klondike, and new ways of extracting gold from ore (such as the cyanide process) made it cheap, and with cheap gold came higher prices. Thus,

THE GREAT CRYPTOGRAM: FRANCIS BACON'S CIPHER in The SO-CALLED SHAKESPEARE PLAYS.

BY IGNATIUS DONNELLY, Author of "Atlantis: The Antediluvian World," and "Ragnarök: The Age of Fire and Gravel."

"And now I will vnclaspe a Secret booke
And to your quicke conceyuing Discontents
Ile reade you Matter, deepe and dangerous,
As full of perill and aduenturous Spirit,
As to o'er-walke a Current, roaring loud,
On the vnstedfast footing of a Speare."
1st Henry IV., Act I, Sc. 3.

·Chicago;
·New York and London·
R. S. Peale & Company.
1888.

Title page from Donnelly's The Great Cryptogram, *his most well-known book and, like the author, a source of controversy.*

a gold standard became palatable, and the issue Donnelly had persisted in raising seemed, for a decade or two, moot.

Donnelly's position, however, had been consistent and today is once again of interest:

> If silver was remonetized, there are still vastly important questions of government paper money, of an abundant currency, of land, and of transportation. . . . We all believe that metallic currency is a temporary expedient—a relic of barbarism, but so long as either metal is to be used we insist that both be used, because both constitute a larger and more abundant currency. . . . [We must] divorce the idea of money totally from any metallic commodity; to make the measure of values rest entirely upon the . . . power of government. . . . We do not believe in commodity money [whether based on] gold, silver, brass, lead, wheat, or potatoes, but as long as gold is continued to be used, we insist that its ancient colleague, silver, shall be used with it as a matter of justice to the debtor class.

It has been argued that Donnelly saw the monetary policies of the government too much in terms of conspiracies of bankers and international financial speculators, and some critics, like Hofstadter, have sniggered at his fear of the power of such conspiracies. Yet Donnelly knew the legislatures of the period very intimately. Like the reformed drunkard, a reformed machine politician and a reformed agent of commodity speculators can be unusually conscious of the temptations of sin. He knew the potency of money and the pliancy of policy to its requirements. It was not only that he had watched the government of the United States twice go begging to private bankers to support its credit (in the Civil War period when Jay Cooke managed the national bond issues—for a substantial profit—and in 1895 when J. P. Morgan and August Belmont helped Grover Cleveland survive a gold crisis—also for a substantial profit). He knew also that international gold brokers and the holders of gold securities had influenced national policy, year in and year out, and even the less forceful silver interests were occasionally capable of rallying congressional strength to secure fat speculative profits (as they did for a few weeks during and after the passage of the Sherman Silver Purchase Act of 1890). The monetary policy of the United States *was* manipulated during the Grant and Cleveland administrations, and in between, by small groups of powerful men who may have been wise but were certainly not disinterested.

It is not strange that Ignatius Donnelly did not endear himself to these men and their western representatives when he pointed out the porosity of the platitudes with which they justified their manipulation. They, however, controlled the magazines and newspapers of large circulation and saw to it that he was depicted as a crank. It has taken eighty years and much new data to restore something of his reputation.

In his last years Ignatius Donnelly was poor, exhausted, and powerless. But after a squalid start he had achieved dignity, had turned his back upon easy acceptance, and had stood by his principles in a remarkably unprincipled era. There is good evidence to indicate that some of his opponents understood that he was worthy of their respect.

In 1895 Donnelly stepped down as leader of the Farmers Alliance. He returned from the last session of the annual meeting to sit alone, eating dinner, in the dining hall of the Brunswick Hotel in Minneapolis. He was too fat, too scarred, too shabby to be an impressive figure. Then, H. C. Long, the new chief of the Alliance, came into the room and asked him to join many of his old friends and antagonists in the hotel's parlor. There they presented him with a pen. Long said, "May it be used unhesitatingly against the enemies of your cause," and, as Martin Ridge describes the scene: "Before Donnelly could reply, Major J. M. Bowler, who had known him as a political friend and foe for thirty-seven years, also presented him with a gold-headed cane. Donnelly was deeply touched. 'I assure you that I have always tried to do right,' he responded. 'I know I am not infallible.... I am not used to a cane....'"

During the previous year Donnelly had received privately evidence of the personal esteem of the most frequent butt of his polemics against the railroads, James J. Hill, and of his political agent in the Democratic party, Michael Doran. Kate Donnelly had been ill for a long time. In June she died. The grieving Donnelly was crippled with rheumatism. His eldest son, Stan, who had cared for his mother to the point of exhaustion, now required medical care. Ignatius Donnelly was in deep financial trouble; these illnesses had drained his small reserve. In his extremity, not only Hill, through his son-in-law, but Doran as well offered to help. Hard men like these, who had learned contempt for most office seekers and who knew that Donnelly was beyond the reach of their influence even in his extremity, would not have volunteered aid to him unless he had their respect.

In the summer of 1900 Donnelly, with sixty-eight years of experience behind him, was having trouble getting through his speeches in support of the Democratic presidential ticket headed by Bryan. He noted that though "my hair is not yet gray... my legs are weak." Just as the new year began, on the morning of January 1, 1901, he died. His pallbearers were "some of the most distinguished business and political leaders of Minnesota—some of whom had been his bitterest political enemies." Chief among them were Senator Moses E. Clapp and Governor John Lind.

It is well to remember him as he was at the peak of his career, in the 1880s, as described by Major Newson:

> Mr. Donnelly looks and acts like a young Falstaff, with a round, chubby face, a round, well-developed body, and round, chubby hands.... one not knowing him would take him to be a jolly bishop.... As a man he is very social... bubbling over with good humor and anecdote.... his hearty laugh is like the cholera, very contagious.... In debate he is a stubborn, able, political opponent; fearless... and decided in his convictions; remarkably ready in repartee and inexhaustible in resources....

Donnelly was a man whose hopes for wealth and eminence had died early, a man who had seen crops turn brown and shrivel in drought years and ripe wheat consumed by locusts. He was an outsider who lost more efforts at office than ten men might have tried, and though he had passed through a dreary period as a member of a corrupt machine, his generous instincts, combative temper, and unwillingness to accept conventional wisdom when it was false had made him a hero to the farmers he led.

Perhaps we have been too hasty in dismissing Ziff's description of Donnelly as romantic. The word "romantic" here denotes a man who insists upon his own vision of the world and of himself though he might be alone in that insistence. This stance does not become less romantic because the world is wrong in its opinions and the solitary dissenter is right.

Ignatius Donnelly persisted in his belief that the emperor had no clothes. All about him journalists and politicians were offering reassurance to the extraordinarily smug beneficiaries of the profusion of the frontier's harvest. Donnelly saw that beneath the apprehension of these fortunate ones, the farmers and the city workers were growing more desperate every day. Others who briefly caught a glimpse of the truth and said so repented their lapse of taste, joined the chorus of acclaim, and were well paid in money and position. But Ignatius Donnelly spent the last years of his life not only insisting on what he believed to be the truth but insisting as well that those with the power to rectify injustice should do so. He saw within the castles of red stone—lit by flaring stained glass, an abundance of rich stuffs, marvelously carven woods and silken hangings, good wines, and the exquisite sauces—the rewards of those who insisted that all was well. Yet, loving luxury and equipped with the taste to savor what they merely owned, he still spoke the unprofitable truth.

Some critics have found it amusing to quote Donnelly's exclamation that he was proud to be the "one man proclaiming truth year after year" even though few listened. "One man clothed in the armor of a righteous cause . . . all the hosts of error . . ."—these were unfashionable modes of expression. Plays like *Inherit the Wind* have sought to make those who used these biblical accents seem silly, but William Jennings Bryan and Ignatius Donnelly were, in their prime, contending for justice against hosts of error and larger hosts of indifference. It is pleasant for well-fed urban liberals to chortle over rural reformers grown old, depicted without dignity upon the stage. But in the days of their long, sweaty struggle to bring justice to the Middle West, these men were giants. In the armor of a righteous cause—despite their lapses and their excesses—they are proof, even today, against the derision of their detractors.

Frank B. Kellogg, who went through life like "a swan, moving without strain about a warm pond in a formal garden, never making a ripple so large as to be unseemly."

II

SOUTHWARD FROM IGNATIUS DONNELLY'S HEADQUARTERS at Nininger, across seventy miles of glacial moraine, across green-tufted mounds ringed with yellow where the rain and wind had worn through to limestone, there is a shallow, sloping river valley deep with brown soil. From a rugged pioneer farmstead in that valley, there came a constituent of Donnelly's who became the urbane and celebrated statesman, Frank Billings Kellogg.

He was twenty-eight years younger than Donnelly, and his timing was better. Donnelly had come west to get rich, had failed during one depression, struggled upward, failed in another, and had become the tribune of the impoverished farmers. Kellogg went west as a child in a poor family; he knew the savage prairie winter and the August heat that presses down upon crops and men and cattle, and bleaches the earth to grey dust. As soon as he could, he escaped to town to become a corporation lawyer. He was lucky in his relatives, and the business cycle was kind to him, and he was a virtuoso of the main chance.

Kellogg was as vain as Donnelly, but instead of permitting vanity to make him a maverick, he learned to adjust—adjust and be gracious—to fit in. Donnelly required the cheers of the populace; Kellogg preferred the quiet approbation of the elegant. Donnelly lived leaping up waterfalls, falling and leaping again. Kellogg was a swan, moving without strain about a warm pond in a formal garden, never making a ripple so large as to be unseemly.

For many years Donnelly and the young Kellogg were near neighbors, and later their public careers overlapped for twenty years. But I have found no comment by either upon the other. By coincidence, however, they were each given a decisive nudge in opposite directions in the same year by Cushman Kellogg Davis, who knew and made use of them both.

Davis had spoiled Donnelly's chance of defeating Alexander Ramsey for the United States Senate in 1875 but had done so with such subtlety that Donnelly supported Davis's successful campaign for that office in 1887. The next year Davis deputized Congressman John Lind to assure Donnelly that if he would campaign for the Republican ticket, "your claims for recognition at the hands of the party will not be ignored." Donnelly was persuaded, even though he was warned of a trap by flinty Knute Nelson, then a backcountry Scandinavian lawyer: "The people who encourage you will do nothing for you. . . . the Yankee blue bloods of the Twin Cities would never tolerate that a damned Norwegian without boodle should ever aspire to the U.S. senatorship, and you will before you are much older realize that an Irishman without boodle will be in the same fix." Nelson was right. Donnelly was treated as a turncoat, got little Republican support, and in the winter of 1889, wrote out of his humiliation and despair his terrible revolutionary vision *Caesar's Column.* (Nelson, who knew how to assay the times and trusted no man, was elected governor in 1892, senator in 1895, and remained solidly in power until his death twenty-eight years later.)

After mouse-trapping Donnelly, Davis took steps to shore up his position by bringing into his law firm his bustling young cousin, Frank Kellogg, who had been practicing law and politics in southern Minnesota. Kellogg had emulated Davis, cross-ruffing the public reform of political incidentals and the private advocacy of the essential interests of corporations. He had won a lawsuit against a flagging railroad company, had been elected city attorney of Rochester, Minnesota, then county attorney, and had been narrowly defeated in an effort to secure the Republican endorsement for attorney general of the state. He had accumulated the friendship and legal business of Rochester's most powerful citizens, including the Doctors Mayo. In 1887 he was ready for the big city.

Some men train well. Cushman Davis chose a tractable associate. Frank Kellogg had a quick mind, a capacity for persistence in small things, and that sententious manner, that implication of rectitude, which was becoming preferred to wit among lawyers in the self-conscious cities of the West. The tutelage of Davis would aid him to go all the way to the senate, the secretaryship of the state, and the Nobel Prize.

Kellogg's authorized and dutiful biographer, David Bryn-Jones, commences his story by floating it upon the current of an "essential . . . part of the American tradition, the story of the poor boy who achieves fame." Kellogg was proud to say that his life was "a remarkable example of the 'log cabin to White House' history." In the Congressional Record he rejoiced that "I was born in the country, started to practice in a little country town in southern Minnesota, and traveled over the prairies of the West trying lawsuits, and I know that many, if not most, of the great lawyers of the United States have come from country towns." Rochester, the market center in which he practiced, was, he said, "an unknown village on the fringe of a far-flung empire . . . destined to become a great, rich country traversed by lines of railroads and dotted with opulent cities. . . ." He saw no romance in the wilderness, no beauty in unturned earth. The frontier, he said, was "beckoning to the ambitious youth and promising golden returns," and the frontier kept its promises to him.

His childhood was classic. He grew up in Adirondack villages; there were, he recalled, "only three or four Democrats in St. Lawrence County . . . and no one knew who they were." When he was nine, his family moved west, by team and wagon, lake steamship, sleeper-less train, ferry, another sleeper-less train, another lake steamship, another train, another steamship, another train, a river steamer, then, as he remembered, by a work train from the Mississippi shore to Eyota, thirteen miles east of Rochester, where the track ran out.

> It was raining and snowing when we got there, and there was no hotel, but there was a store that had a loft over it. . . . my father, my mother, my brother, my sister, and myself . . . all bunked on the floor. . . . there was a board across a chair, and as I was tired and sleepy . . . I sat down on one end of it. The other end flew up in the air and a kerosene lamp that was on it was smashed in pieces, leaving us in complete darkness.

In later years, amid candle-lit splendor in his London mansion, having dined with the king and golfed with the Prince of Wales, he could recall that night in Eyota.

On the morning after their arrival a neighbor from their home town in New York brought them to the hamlet of Viola by oxteam and wagon. There Frank slept with his brother in the attic, often shaking off the snow that drifted in through the shingles. That was the winter of 1865–1866. Ignatius Donnelly was in his second term in Congress, still the youngest member of the House. The Kelloggs were his typical constituents, single-crop wheat farmers. "Not much was heard in Olmstead County about rotation of crops or diversified farming," Kellogg later recalled.

The Kelloggs were poor. Frank wanted to become a lawyer and always regretted that he had had no formal education after he left school in 1873, in his fourteenth year. That was the winter that Minnesota weather again left its mark in his mind. He had taken a sleigh-load of wheat to the river port of Minneiska and had returned, as usual, up the deep-riven, oak-thicketed valley, to reach the prairie plateau at Elgin. Joe Richardson, a neighbor, warned him that there was a blizzard on the way, but he kept loading four-foot lengths of firewood to take home and, late in the day, started home in the face of the lashing snow. A search party found him at ten o'clock that night stuck in a snowdrift. He had walked twenty miles.

Kellogg was small and muscular, capable of great exertions and steely self-discipline. Minnesota winter provides a constant incentive to get rich enough to be warm in winter, and the drudgery of a frontier farm drove Kellogg to seek out the "golden returns" of the city. He was tough; he took no more risks than were absolutely necessary; and he put behind himself any feeling of companionship in the struggles and privations of the single-crop farmer. Good luck reinforced his upward striving while misfortune forced Ignatius Donnelly back down each time he sought prosperity, and it seems likely that there was in these two men a disposition toward divergent lives. Donnelly actually preferred swimming upstream; Kellogg caught the current of his time and rode upon it.

As soon as he could, Kellogg left the farm and began learning the law in the office of a Norwegian immigrant named H. A. Eckholdt. He milked cows and worked on neighboring farms to earn his keep: fifty cents a day during seeding, a dollar at harvest time. He later recalled that by "intense application" he learned enough Latin and law to pass his examinations; then by "strict economy and hard work I managed to earn a living in my chosen profession."

Kellogg customarily applied to himself the prefabricated phrases of the rags-to-riches myth. He was not imaginative, and it is likely that even if it had not been useful to him politically to clothe himself in these phrases, he might still have found it comfortable to buy a biography off the rack. Others recorded that during this period he was widening the space between himself and his boyhood associates by serving as a collection agent for farm machinery companies, traveling "over the prairies of the West" in search of payments on delinquent notes. It was these same companies that were the least fastidious in employing any means necessary to dissuade the legislature from adopting Donnelly's restraints on their usurious interest rates.

Kellogg knew how hard life was on the prairie farm, how exposed the farmers were to blizzard, to price manipulation and rail rate discrimination, to falsified weights and grading; and he wanted to depart from such a squalid scene in all haste. Thirty years after he left the farm forever, he was willing to bestow upon his Senate colleagues an unusually self-congratulatory recital of his career, emphasizing the delights of life on a farm, but his speeches warmed considerably as he recalled the "golden returns" in the "opulent cities."

> The concentration of wealth, the marvelous accomplishments of science and invention, the increase in manufacture and world commerce, and the increase in communication and rapid transportation have afforded opportunities in the cities for large incomes, the amassing of great fortunes, and that, together with the attractiveness of city life, have taken from the farm much of the best blood of the nation.

There is, of course, nothing strange in a desire to avoid the unpleasant and seek riches and "attractiveness," but Kellogg harbored the delusion all his life that, despite his rejection of farm life, he was nonetheless still capable of understanding and speaking for the farmer. He truly regarded himself, as Harold Ickes once described Wendell L. Willkie, a simple "barefoot Wall Street lawyer." He repeatedly employed a formula about the farmer in his recorded public addresses: reverence for "the supreme importance . . . of agriculture. In all times the prosperity and greatness of the nations of the world have been based upon agricultural pursuits . . . independent proprietors of the soil . . . the small farmer, the owner of the soil. . . ." He could even borrow a Bryanesque turn of phrase on the right occasion, to contrast the yeoman and the city dweller: "The degeneration which is going on in the centers of population, like our large cities, is a terrible drain upon our nation, which is being made good from the blood, sinew, and brain of the land. . . . Show me a nation whose agriculture declines and I will show you a decadent nation."

But his attitude toward the farmer was that of the city creditor. He was opposed to "radical measures" to aid the farmer. His rhetoric about "independent yeomen" did not seduce him into advocating expenditures to sustain the national bucolic museum he portrayed. He was always opposed to "men who are seeking . . . radical legislation": Populists, La Follette Progressives, or draftsmen of New Deal farm policies. He knew that "the farmers of Minnesota . . . have turned radical because of the prices of their products," but "all this twaddle about controlled inflation is nonsense"—this during a period of sharply declining farm prices. The seven-year-long farm depression of the 1920s and 1930s was, he thought, merely a panic, and it could be cured by "thrift and industry." His response to the ancient association of low prices, high debt, and deflationary policy was, as in all things, conventional. He was for hard work and "stabilizing the dollar." Whatever temporary distress could not be alleviated by thrift, would, he grandly assumed, come right in time: "the relative value of farm products and other products will eventually be worked out and adjusted through economic forces." He was proud that his own "conservative" measures as a senator prevented the "very radical legislation" advocated by George Norris and others to increase exports and elevate farm prices. The wisdom of these measures was not at issue. That they were "radical" was enough for him.

Kellogg had commenced his career forty years earlier. The great boom of the 1880s was getting underway, and during its upward surge he was carried along. Then, when he needed an additional boost, he sought out Cousin Cushman to help him

Kellogg had come a long way from the schoolhouse he had attended on the frontier, when he visited it in 1922, below; among other things, he had achieved familiarity with those whom the times considered great men—like Calvin Coolidge, seen with Kellogg above. Such things were important.

through a difficult lawsuit, and he got the boost. He afterward spoke of "the life struggle of a boy in the simple . . . surroundings of the north country . . . and [his] rise to fame," of his own "interesting career." He congratulated himself as having been one of those who, "self-reliant, vigorous in body, trained in hardy schools, inspired by ambition," had achieved success in the city. He was proud to recall that once he had been "grubbing out a living on a frontier farm," but his recollection aroused no fervent feeling of kinship for those still at it. He was delighted to have come so far from all that, from all "them."

He had difficulty understanding why "they" did not regard such a paragon with the enthusiasm of the paragon himself; one reason may be that they perceived his patronizing attitude. Of the laboring classes he said in a campaign speech, "If we should have them make good American citizens, educate their children, and be an element of stability in the nation, they must be treated justly and have their fair share of the products of their labor." But woe be unto those who would seek by direct political action to improve their lot, who listened to "the fomentations of the radicals." "Revolutionary propaganda" of their kind "stirs the muddy waters of discontent." He made little effort at rectifying the causes of discontent. "Time," he intoned, "cures many things."

Kellogg carried over into his public policies a smug sense of separation between those who were feckless or improvident toilers and those who were splendid and successful like himself. During the depression he was glad he could "hang on to . . . good stocks" and observed with a curl of the lip former colleagues who were not of the elite; of a destitute lawyer friend he said, "He has always been improvident. Nevertheless it is a rather sad situation for a man to arrive at his age and with it nothing to do. . . . we have to help a poor devil who is on the wrong side." (Charles Cleaver, Kellogg's percipient critic, has underlined the Calvinist implications of that final damning phrase.) Kellogg could use the same tone about a retired foreign service officer in those days before pensions: "The government doesn't owe him a living, but I am sorry for him nevertheless."

In 1930, as a director of the First National Bank of St. Paul—then an institution of unchallenged supremacy in the region, dominating its competitors—he urged his colleagues to retire from any broad responsibility: "What is the object of our running a sound and conservative bank when we are assessed to pay the debts of rotten banks which have been recklessly managed?" From the battlements he looked out upon other, less-endowed institutions whose depositors were losing the savings of a lifetime, and he alone, it is said, voted at a directors meeting against a weekend's loan to keep another bank afloat while government funds, guaranteed by the Treasury Department, were on their way.

The response of a man of this sort to the next decade was predictable. He was for a sharp cutback in governmental expenditure and vehemently opposed to any large program of relief. He admonished those who could not "sell some bonds" or "keep ... good stocks" to await the beneficent workings of the economic forces which had, forty years earlier, helped to make him rich. "Congress cannot legislate prosperity," he said, and it should neither try to encourage it nor to succor the victims of its absence. "Readjustments must come through the natural result of economic forces.... The great principles of supply and demand will take care of prices and production." Relief measures might erode "individual energy and enterprise," and he deplored them. "We are not wards of the government." Certainly he was not. "We are self-reliant, energetic, and resourceful people.... the American people must help themselves.... The main reliance is the generosity and the public spirit of the American people."

David Bryn-Jones, Kellogg's biographer made use of his subject's private papers and was never critical of his benefactor. But at one point he said of the young Kellogg:

> He did not have then, nor has he had since, "a minority temperament." ... Later he would shape a personal philosophy, or find one, which would justify what at first was an instinctive reaction. He believed with Edmund Burke that loyalty to "one's own platoon" is one of the conditions of loyalty to those larger entities which claim man's allegiance.

Is there a rock showing through the smooth-flowing sorghum? Does the biographer wish to tell us something? Kellogg was not one of those given to inconvenient personal loyalties. His loyalties were larger—to a "platoon." His platoon was amply endowed and willing to reward such loyalty. It merely required that one be adaptable.

Kellogg was adaptable. Impressionable, in fact. His private correspondence shows him glorying in dinner, golf, or a carriage ride with a celebrity, warmed by the consoling proximity of the rich (to borrow a phrase from F. Scott Fitzgerald) and heedful of the opinions of the titled in ways which would be touching in a debutante but pathetic in a middle-aged secretary of state. Politically, he moved from the gravitational field of one great man to that of another, and his own orbit bent to accommodate them. Ideologically, he called himself a Progressive, but he was as ready to move backward as forward with the opinions of his platoon.

The degree to which he was not only loyal to, but a prisoner of, that platoon appeared in the last decade of his life when he was certain that its attitudes toward Franklin Roosevelt were representative of the populace. "In this part of the country it is hard to find a real Roosevelt supporter. The extravagance and waste of this administration are generally condemned. . . . The people are sick and tired of those professional 'brain trusters' and of all the fool experiments of this administration. In my opinion it would be just simply a 'picnic' to carry Minnesota for the Republicans at the present time." A few months later Roosevelt defeated Alf Landon by a landslide.

He resented the efforts of "agitators" to "stir up" criticism of the prevailing order. In the 1920s he had responded to Robert La Follette's speeches against the Teapot Dome scandal as Alexander Ramsey's friends responded, in the 1870s, to Ignatius Donnelly's attacks on scandals of the Grant Administration. "I am mortified beyond measure that a few men greedy of riches and one or two currupt officials can not only damage a great—I might say—two great political parties and encourage radicalism, but can destroy public confidence in the business of the country. . . . That is no excuse for the Senate to make a spectacle of itself like a ranting, scandal-mongering old woman. . . ."

It was not the crime but the consequences of its exposure which seemed to bother him the most. In the same way he was offended by La Follette's angry attacks upon the Supreme Court after it had twice set aside efforts to regulate child labor. The Court, which was intent upon the preservation of property rights and what it called "freedom of contract," had stood athwart efforts of reformers from Donnelly's time through La Follette's to improve working conditions and protect children from exploitation. Kellogg never evidenced sympathy with the children, but he was out at daybreak in full armor to protect the Court against "agitators who are going up and down the land denouncing the Supreme Court and the Constitution." La Follette's "pernicious doctrines," in 1922, "strike at the very foundation of constitutional government."

Two years later he wrote his partner that he did not believe that "the American people can be carried away with such demagoguery and quack remedies and revolutionary tendencies as La Follette represents." There was some snobbery in his description of La Follette's Minnesota manager: "a man without any standing" in whose shipper's bureau "there is not a single shipper of any importance"—definitely not one of the platoon.

His emphasis upon "extravagance" and "thrift" arouses curiosity about the psychological basis of his conservatism. He was not conservative out of reverence for the past; he was not contemplative nor scholarly; he felt no stirring of ancient sympathies nor reverence for ancient institutions. Nor was he a conservative out of pessimism; he believed that "sound economic laws of a permanent character" would lead inevitably to progress. He was, instead, a retentive character, made anxious by change and relying upon riches—which he called "resources"—to provide comfort and stability. When World War I called for extraordinary exertions, he said, "It is necessary in times like these to conserve our resources." In another speech he said, with some passion, "We must watch carefully the burdens we place upon our people so that we may be able with our resources—our splendid resources—to meet any of the exigencies which may arise in this unfortunate struggle."

This was the rather short man with a noble face and an even nobler crop of prematurely white hair (much the same nobility as John Bricker's) who rose rags-to-riches to a seat in the United States Senate in 1916 as a Progressive and, finally, became an international figure as the secretary of state who assembled the nations of the world to sign the Kellogg-Briand Peace Pact in 1928. How could such a man have such a reputation? How was all this possible for one in whose voluminous writings no granule of wit can be found, in whose interminable public speeches no fresh phrase, no original concept lightens the relentless redundancy?

At the outset one wonders how he came to be known as a Progressive. The term itself had a range of meanings. Kellogg's was on the cool or blue end of the Progressive spectrum, which advocated those reforms which had already become respectable. William Allen White knew many corporation lawyers like Kellogg, who were willing to accept an old Populist idea which had "shaved its whiskers, washed its shirt, put on a derby, and moved up into the middle of the class—the upper-middle class." Like White himself and Theodore Roosevelt, they took Populist proposals, blunted their edges, placed them in gift-wrapping of bright language, and made them attractive to a majority of the public. Wisconsin's Robert M. La Follette and Minnesota's Governor John A. Johnson, who were keeping score on the practical results rather than the rhetoric, noted that the Roosevelt-Kellogg Progressives "filled the air with noise and smoke, which confused and obscured the line of action, but when . . . quiet was restored, it was always a matter of surprise that so little had really been accomplished."

Tactically, Kellogg was perfectly fitted to benefit from the decline of potency in Minnesota's reform movement, which followed the deaths of Donnelly in 1901 and Johnson in 1909. He could serve the oligarchs and at the same time pose as a log-cabin-reared son of the soil. In a state still rent by antipathies among citizens, two-thirds of whom were first- or second-generation Americans, he was of old Yankee stock. He had an additional advantage: a chloroform dignity which quieted questioners. He could do so without hypocrisy because he apparently was so intent upon his own rise to riches that he was blind to the present injustices which still occupied the attention of "radicals."

What was Kellogg's real attitude toward the trusts? He secured political advancement as a "trust buster" but was always a devout advocate and companion of the proprietors of what the public meant by "trusts." Was his the view of the matter expressed by Mr. Dooley? "Th' trusts are heejus monsters built up be th' inlightened intherprise if th' men that have done so much to advance progress in our beloved counthry. On wan hand I wud stamp thim under fut; on th' other hand, not so fast."

Justice tempered with convenience. Kellogg stated his hardly passionate adherence to reform in his famous speech as president of the American Bar Association: "In the enactment and enforcement of those laws called for by a progressive people, lawyers should be statesmen.... If we do this... we may maintain our influence in the councils of state and nation; and we may aid in shaping progressive legislation and add immeasurably to the wisdom of government. But if we refuse it will be done without us."

His political career is interesting in its clear expression of the temper of midwestern respectable opinion and also in its demonstration of how Sulla could look like Marius by carefully selecting his adversaries. His first national celebrity came from having successfully occasioned the collapse of the "Paper Trust." As Bryn-Jones admits, "The interests jeopardized in this case, in so far as there was jeopardy, were not those of the weak and impotent, but those of the newspapers and publishing companies capable of putting up a resolute [and expensive] defense." The "trust" was raising prices of newsprint; the publishers raised the cry of "monopoly." Kellogg, as attorney for the publishers, helped bring the prices down again and was compensated not only in cash but in the editorial adulation which led him to his next big case, against E. H. Harriman, lord of the Union Pacific. Harriman was, Bryn-Jones says, "regarded by the public as one of the bold, bad robber barons of the world of dubious finance."

Kellogg's biographer does not go on to say that Harriman was also regarded as a dangerous opponent by one of Kellogg's chief clients, James J. Hill, of the "Northern Roads." Harriman and Hill had been contending for power for twenty years, and Hill was not offended in 1908 when his lawyer was assigned the task of advancing, as special counsel, the Interstate Commerce Commission's efforts to curb Harriman. On the witness stand Harriman made something of the fact that Kellogg was not so fearsome a foe of Hill's combinations as of Harriman's:

> MR. HARRIMAN: You are on two sides of this Mr. Kellogg.
> MR. KELLOGG: Perhaps.
> MR. HARRIMAN: You have just come from Minnesota. You were arguing there the other way.
> MR. KELLOGG: All right; go ahead. You can say anything you please.
> MR. HARRIMAN: I wish I had you on my side.
> MR. KELLOGG: I do not think you need me. Now, Mr. Harriman . . . the evidence, etc.

Kellogg, and Kellogg alone, is the authority for the story that another client, Judge Gary of U.S. Steel, tried to dissuade him from contending with Harriman; that Kellogg offered to resign his counselship for the giant corporation; and that Gary, who, says Bryn-Jones, "formed a truer estimate of him as a result," tore up that paper and the two "remained friends."*

It was Kellogg's next great case—forcing the Rockefeller brothers and their partners to break up the Standard Oil Company into a number of smaller companies—which established him as *the* trust buster. There were three results of the celebrated Standard Oil case. First, where the Sherman Act had proscribed any combination in restraint of trade, Kellogg argued and won the case by inserting the modifier "unreasonable," thereby investing the Supreme Court with the jurisdiction to decide which restraints were reasonable and which were not. Second, it inconvenienced the Rockefellers. Bryn-Jones adds his gloss: "Kellogg . . . labored persistently and courageously. . . . True the problem of the trust remained, and still remains; the problem of the Standard Oil Company remained . . . but at least one important step toward solution had been taken." And, third, Kellogg became a hero. One enthusiastic journalist wrote in 1911: "There is no lawyer in the country whom criminal wealth more fears today."

Kellogg felt that this progressive reputation denied him the

*This is very like Kellogg's story of his refusal to accept appointment to the Senate Foreign Relations Committee at the cost of a promise to support Henry Cabot Lodge. Kellogg related how he told Lodge: "I won't make any promises of that kind. I cannot. I have never made such a promise in my life and am quite sure I never shall." He had a number of such stories.

Kellogg's grandest scheme was that of peace—but not all the hope, good faith, and gentlemen's agreements in the world were enough.

post of secretary of war in President Taft's cabinet, but it did gain him, in 1916, the Republican nomination for the United States Senate, heading off the prospect of a more progressive candidate like Governor Adolph O. Eberhardt or a "radical" like the elder Charles A. Lindbergh. Cushman Davis had taught him the fine art of heading off—of timely adaptation. One can suppose that Kellogg was less aware of his footwork than the cynical old master, but he was capable of very intricate maneuvers. In the years 1910 to 1912, for example, he retained the friendship of William Howard Taft and of Theodore Roosevelt. Roosevelt, in voluntary exile in Africa, was in frequent correspondence with Kellogg, asking his judgment "on the political situation in the West." At the same time, Kellogg could walk frequently in the rose garden with Taft. Archie Butt, who was present on one such stroll, reported that Kellogg advocated to Taft the withholding of patronage appointments to Roosevelt's friends in the West and that he gave Taft "a full account . . . as he described it, of 'The Back from Elba Plot'" to return Roosevelt to these flowery precincts as occupant of the White House.

Kellogg joined another walk-out of the Republican Convention in 1912, where he had unsuccessfully supported Roosevelt's disputed delegates against Taft's, but he handled the matter so subtly that he received a telegram from Taft on the next day saying, "A thousand thanks my dear Kellogg. . . . I know how much you personally had to do with the admirable results of the convention." Taft, of course, was in Washington, away from the convention, and had a poor political intelligence service.

It is impossible to make consistency out of Kellogg's senatorial career. He introduced numerous agricultural bills of apparently conflicting purposes—some, it appears, from a fear that "it will be done without us." He was one of a number of moderate senators who swung back and forth like water in a ship's bilge as the debate on the League of Nations tilted first one way and then the other. In 1922 he was denied the reelection which Folwell says "he had a good right to expect" by the new Farmer-Labor coalition. President Harding then sent him to the Conference of American States in Chile and later appointed him ambassador to the Court of St. James.

Kellogg went to Europe with prejudices about nations neatly

divided, hermetically sealed within their boundaries. Each seemed to him to have a distinctive and, apparently, homogeneous character. He respected men who "know the Mexicans" or "understand the Chinese." He already "knew" the Germans: "The Hun has not changed in two thousand years. Civilization may have sharpened his lust for conquest and power, and knowledge and science increased his instruments of destruction, but he is a Hun at heart. . . ." The British, on the other hand, are "polite . . . have tremendous courage . . . are mighty jealous of their commerce." Later, as secretary of state, he was glad that "Poindexter wired me . . . that the Peruvians are particularly susceptible to 'palaver' and very responsive to treatment which they describe by the word 'simpatico.'" The Montenegrins were "hardy"; the French and Italians derived their vitality from the fact that they are an agricultural people.

These were the conventional attitudes of his platoon; despite his great opportunities, he did not enlarge his thinking. Speaking of Germans as Huns or France as prosperous because it is "a working country" was enough to gratify a luncheon club audience, and Kellogg asked little more understanding of himself than that. He apparently believed that nations are discrete entities, each having its own character. Perhaps it was because he wanted each nation to "develop its own nationality" that he said in the middle 1930s that Hitler merely "needed a good spanking" but was not a serious threat to peace. "I haven't taken this talk about war in Europe very seriously. It seems to me that Hitler is rattling sabers and strutting up and down the platform largely for the benefit of Germany. . . . When you stop and think about it, what has Germany got to go to war about?"

By that time, of course, Kellogg was known as the proponent of the Kellogg-Briand Peace Pact, in which sixty-two nations solemnly renounced war as an instrument of national policy. He wished this treaty to serve as his testament. It has been roughly treated by critics as diverse as Drew Pearson, who wrote a book to prove that it was a good idea but not Kellogg's, and George F. Kennan, who regarded it as a prime example of that "legalistic-moralistic" approach to foreign policy which made it difficult for American secretaries of state between the two great wars to deal forthrightly with specific power problems.

The evidence seems fairly plain that Kellogg was skeptical about such a treaty when it was proposed as an exchange of assurances only between France and the United States. He was still resistant when a number of articulate peace groups took up and broadened the idea to include all nations. His memoranda to President Coolidge cautioned against accepting the idea; he wrote Elihu Root that "there is a tremendous demand in this country ... for the so-called outlawry of war. Nobody knows just what that means." But as more and more petitions came across his desk, together with enthusiastic letters from prominent platoon leaders, and even Senator Borah was ready to persuade the Foreign Affairs Committee that it was a "noble idea," Kellogg began to concede. After the committee, under Borah's urging, recommended the treaty, Kellogg made it his own and fought for its passage. There can be no doubt that he came to believe that it would have a "moral effect ... upon the peoples of the world," that it would make it more difficult for nations once again to go to war.

It had additional virtues from his point of view. It required no radical measures like that "framework of supergovernment," that internationalism "of some extreme, impractical dreamer," which he had feared at the time of the League of Nations debate. It had no enforcement procedures, could upset no one, and make no demands for a change in the established ways of doing international business. It "must depend upon the good faith of nations." Raised as he had been in a frontier society where there was a desire by respectable people to establish "law and order" as quickly and firmly as possible, in which property rights were exchanged by contract and where everybody believed both in contracts and in property, he found it easy to believe that international society was like that, too. Treaty obligations, he thought, "are as sacred as the private obligations which arise between man and man. ... they lie as the very foundation of peace and good order. ..." There were those who wanted some things more than law and order—those who would use his treaty as a cover for their preparation for war. Self-righteous, narrow in vision, he persuaded many of his countrymen that they could rest secure while such a treaty set forth the rules. Meanwhile, Hitler, Mussolini, and Stalin prepared for a game without rules.

Frank Billings Kellogg was a celebrity and, in his lifetime, a popular hero. He carried into international affairs a set of assumptions which might have had some value to some Minnesota magnates during prosperous times but were dangerous delusions in a larger world. He discouraged tough deterrence of real threats to peace by his insistence that words and signatures were enough. "The moral influence of an idea," he said, "is greater than the power of armaments in maintaining peace."

Kellogg, suave and sanctimonious, could not understand why Winston Churchill said in 1932: "I cannot recall any time when the gap between the kind of words which statesmen used and what was actually happening in many countries was so great as it is now." There had always been that gap in Frank Kellogg's life. He was lucky that it never closed in upon him.

Ignatius Donnelly had an apocalyptic vision of terror in the streets, bloodshed, and the destruction of luxury in a revolt of the landless and comfortless. Kellogg could see no such dangers abroad or at home. Such forebodings were the agitation of a crank. Kellogg was well and the world was well. He was content and the world must be content. He was a creature of easy rectitude, knowing apparently no agony of conscience, no doubt about the society which had rewarded him so amply. On his upward path he went surrounded by his own cocoon of satisfaction. He cannot fairly be called brave, for he never suffered from a conviction which was not accepted by powerful men about him. He had intelligence and energy. He had among the men of his platoon a reputation for being a practical man, though he, and they, were working in clay on the brink of a volcano.

Chapter Six

F. Scott Fitzgerald

William Gray Purcell

I

THOUGH THE STACK OF BOOKS ON F. Scott Fitzgerald gets higher and higher, Arthur Mizener's biography, now nearly twenty years old, stays on top. There are a number of reasons for its preeminence, including its dignity of style, but among them the most important are two insights: first, that Fitzgerald was only incidentally and by happenstance the "laureate of the Jazz Age," and second, that his distinction as a writer was his grace in expressing what he had seen with a very sharp eye. He reported what he observed in lucid and lovely prose, but he was not an imaginative writer. He did not seek to create for his characters or for himself a different mold. As Mizener put it: "He always . . . wrote about himself or about people and things with which he was intimate. As a consequence his life is inextricably bound up with his work."

When Fitzgerald died in 1940, Westbrook Pegler and other grave dancers spoke about the departed as if he had been a male flapper. Pegler called him the leader of a pack of "undisciplined and self-indulgent brats" during the extinct twenties and implied that he had spent all his life as one of a "cult of crying drunks . . . sniffling about the sham and tinsel of it all." Actually, of course, Fitzgerald represented and reported a period far longer and more interesting than the Jazz Age; he was publishing before 1920, and his best work was done during the thirties, after the Jazz Age had strangled itself on ticker tape.

Fitzgerald wrote about what he experienced. His life was a quarry from which he cut chunks of material and then made stories of it. Some of them were exquisitely polished and shaped; some were rough and ungainly, executed when he was tired, harried, or drunk. He wrote about his youth in St. Paul and White Bear Lake in the years before the First World War; about his experiences at the St. Paul Academy, the Cardinal Newman school, and at Princeton during the Edwardian years; about the war (or, rather, about not being in the war), then about the Jazz Age, and then about what it was like to be middle-aged, broken in health and spirit, and irrelevant during the proletarian thirties. Finally, he made a new start and wrote about big business and show business in Hollywood.

Mizener and later biographers have made all this quite clear. But there still lingers a misapprehension which is as serious as type-casting Fitzgerald as a golden boy of the twenties, that is, considering him a romantic. *Time* magazine called him "the last romantic," and Allen Tate has been quoted as saying: "it was his very romanticism which kept him from ever learning more about the American rich than a little boy knows about cowboys and Indians."

But if the term "romantic" means anything at all, it describes a person whose imagination is powerful enough to lead him to live within an atmosphere of his own creation, somewhat apart from the real world. If a romantic is a strong character, as Don Quixote and Giacomo Beltrami were, he can remain impervious to the world's derision or disbelief. If he is stronger still, he can, at least for a while, make the world provide materials to make tangible what he imagines. This is what a great architect or painter or politician can do. If he is weaker, he can withdraw into his dreams.

But the romantic does not, like Fitzgerald, remain locked in a lifelong dance with the real world, his senses all responding to its reality. The romantic does not mold autobiographical fiction out of molten sensation. Fitzgerald could not escape the world of the real present except by moving a short distance

F. Scott Fitzgerald, wrongly cast as a romantic, was in truth a realist who limned the details of the world he knew with precise observation.

backward into the realities of his own past. If he did hide some aspects of his past behind a scrim of golden words, that was because he wrote so beautifully, not because he was a writer of romance. Even his most fantastic stories, like "The Diamond as Big as the Ritz" are mosaics of precisely observed details, in that case of a Montana ranch he visited and, perhaps, of estates like the Vanderbilts' Biltmore. When he did blow a soap bubble of imagined grandeur, he always collapsed it at the end of the story and returned his characters to the pavement. Romantics do not do that.

The most important component of the romantic tradition was not important to Fitzgerald: that is the dimension of reverence for certain great mysteries, for nature, for God, for the dimly known past. In American Romanticism, there has been a consistent theme of faith in the potentialities of men—men in general. Among Fitzgerald's contemporaries the contemplative romantics directed their lives according to that faith and with respect for those mysteries. Among them was another artist who made new and beautiful things out of materials quarried from midwestern realities, the architect William Gray Purcell. He walked the same streets as Fitzgerald, knew some of the same people, but he, not Fitzgerald, stands in the great romantic tradition. This is said not to denigrate Fitzgerald but to encourage a reappraisal of his role as an observer and reporter of aspects of the midwestern experience which preceded the Jazz Age and which were far more important in his life than that transitory time. It is also said to give some greater recognition of what the romantic tradition contributed to the architecture of the Middle West, since the architecture of Purcell's era is the region's proudest artistic achievement.

Sharpening a contrast between the two men may heighten an understanding of both. Focus on their attitude toward money. Rudyard Kipling described the Middle West as a place where the people go about talking loudly through their noses about money, and it is certainly true that money is a popular subject. This is, of course, not limited to that region in any extraordinary degree, for money is occasionally discussed even in Boston. But, perhaps, in places where a great deal of it appears on the scene rather suddenly, it has a special interest.

That interest was, for Fitzgerald, a fascination. But it was not uncritical or diffuse. It was a concentrated interest in a peculiar kind of money used in particular ways. Fitzgerald's fascination was with money used for spending. He did not care about money as a medium of exchange or as an instrument of social policy or as a lever for personal power. He observed and reported its use as a miraculous agent to create an appreciative environment. Coins scattered about became bright mirrors, and if the Jazz Age was reported by him especially well, it was because the Jazz Age was an orgy of pecuniary narcissism.*

Money worked marvels in the Middle West. The generation that was young during the depression after 1893 and that reached maturity as the economy swelled toward the "greatest, gaudiest spree in history" were especially conscious of it. Fitzgerald was the spokesman of that midwestern generation in this respect at least. He was not a regional writer in the same sense as Faulkner; much of the action he described took place on Long Island or the Riviera or Hollywood, but the forces moving that action came out of the prairie and the new cities of the great central valley of America. More than that. Those forces were set in motion at a peculiar time when those cities were settling down and their affluent inhabitants were spending the harvest of the Midwest's frontier.

The pecuniary bias which could be expected in any middle-class environment was intensified in his time and place by a tension between a continuing expectation of a frontier bonanza and the rather sudden shattering of that expectation in the somber, threadbare realities of the post-frontier period. Frederick Jackson Turner pronounced, three years before Fitzgerald's birth, that the frontier had passed. America, he said, would no longer have available "a wilderness at the edge . . . open . . . to all who with strong arms and stout heart desired to hew out a home and a career for themselves." Walter Prescott Webb, Turner's most eloquent disciple, writing for Fitzgerald's generation, expressed the frontier's anticipation in other terms. Webb set forth the alternation of expectation and disappointment

*It is a convenience, though not a coincidence, that the greatest buildings designed by Purcell and by his colleagues George Elmslie and Louis Sullivan were midwestern banks.

which runs through so many of Fitzgerald's stories:

> The frontier was a land in which Mother Nature had hidden many Easter eggs, many prizes. Just as the children hunt after the Easter eggs have all been found, so do men with an Easter egg psychology.... So it is with men in search of fortunes.... The modern man cannot divest himself of his desire to act in the old way. The result is an offset between his desires and his possibilities. The cogs of his mind do not engage with reality, and therefore he is out of gear.... he is living in the realm of unreality, a land of remembered things. He is trying to harness the dreams of yesterday, of the frontier, to the machines of today and tomorrow.

Many of Fitzgerald's characters seem to live in this "realm of unreality," this state of perpetual expectation and constant disappointment. They were beautiful, entrancing, glamorous, rich, and damned. Fitzgerald's special interest was in the association between their peculiar beauty—which was the beauty of riches, of sunlight on gold, of voices "full of money"—and their doom.

During the proletarian thirties, Fitzgerald was criticized for writing so much about the rich. It was said, he admitted, that "my material was such as to preclude all dealing with mature persons in a mature world." His anguished reply was: "My God! It was my material, and it was all I had to deal with." It was, indeed, material of his own time, but he selected it, rejecting much else that was equally available. His pattern of selection was the conscious product of his artistic intelligence, but it was also determined by what he had felt and learned in St. Paul between the depression of 1893 and the First World War.

Fitzgerald's work was organized by his interest in the spending of money: its witchery of beauty and its curse. This point may appear more clearly when the material he rejected is examined. For example, he did not write about the great frontier acquirers, of whom the most conspicuous to him, as a son of St. Paul, would have been the railroad builder James J. Hill. Before he wrote *The Great Gatsby,* Fitzgerald told John Chapin Mosher that he had "very deliberately ... taken as the field for his talent the great study of American wealth.... he had made it his business to ferret out how it was cornered." But he never did much ferreting, for in his time "how it was cornered" was far less arresting a subject than how it was spent. Specifically, he had told Mosher, he was engaged in the "serious study" of James J. Hill. But he soon perceived that that study was inappropriate to his own time, when men like Hill had lost much of their independent power, had become "Morganized." The promethean tycoon of the Middle West, the archetypal frontiersman of the previous generation, was already becoming an anachronism, and Fitzgerald the reporter was not interested in history, even recent history.

This change in the paradigmatic quality of men like Hill occurred quite suddenly. In the early 1880s, when the Great Northern was organized and the Northern Pacific reached the West Coast, when Hill and E. H. Harriman and Henry Villard conducted their vendettas on a continental scale, Charles Francis Adams had observed them. They "declared war, negotiated peace, reduced courts, legislatures, and sovereign states to an unqualified obedience to their will, disturbed trade, agitated the currency, imposed taxes, and boldly setting both law and public opinion at defiance, freely exercised many of the attributes of sovereignty."

But in 1889 J. Pierpont Morgan called eighteen railroad presidents together and told them that the old days were over. The rate wars were to end. The sending of snipers to discourage competitive road crews was to stop. The presidents were to consult with each other, and, of course, with him. And they were to heed his advice. The rivalries of the frontier, he said, "were not elsewhere customary in civilized communities, and no good reason exists why such a practice should continue among railroads." Morgan could arrange things in New York. The midwestern tycoon, the great user of money to build empires of lumber or wheat or iron ore or railways, had never before been so easily intimidated. Now the investment banker and the manipulator of trusts prevailed over the empire builder. John D. Rockefeller had already announced that "the day of combination is here to stay. Individualism has gone, never to return." Now he, Andrew Carnegie, and Henry Oliver of Pittsburgh moved in upon the independent iron ore producers of northern Minnesota and brought that region under their sway.

But Fitzgerald, with all his interest in wealth, did not write about the financiers either. They inhabited a world of esoteric finance far removed from what he had himself observed in his place and time. It was said of Fitzgerald by his detractors that he was a courtier to the rich, a sycophant. He never denied that he enjoyed the consoling proximity of the rich, that he rejoiced in the easy skill with which some of them swam through life. But they were not interesting to him only because they were rich. His interest did not, as we have noted, extend to those who used money to dominate whole regions or regulate whole industries. Neither was he curious, as Balzac had been, about the life of the pure accumulator, the man to whom money was its own reward. Fitzgerald knew such men, but he thought rather vaguely that "business is a dull game, and they pay a big price in human values for their money." Balzac had an imaginative capacity to enter into the life of Père Goriot, but Fitzgerald did not.

Though he was criticized for a promiscuous predeliction for the rich, Fitzgerald was very selective. The pure acquisitives, like the financiers, were not his material. They were not representative of his native region; they were creatures, indeed, of the old puritan world from which the frontiersmen had fled, the gray world of sumptuary restraint, of accumulation blessed by the clergy. There were misers in the Middle West, but they had to hold out against the extravagant frontier spirit.

As Fitzgerald was finishing *This Side of Paradise,* his first paean to promiscuous spending and the opulent life, the great philanthropist Andrew Carnegie was dying. Why should Carnegie's type have been as uninteresting to Fitzgerald as tycoons, financiers, and misers had been? Carnegie had an income of twelve million a year—why was he so unpersuasive to Fitzgerald's contemporaries when he asked that the new American rich should "set an example of modest, unostentatious living, shunning display or extravagance"?

Neither acquisition nor philanthropy fitted the mood of the Middle West in Fitzgerald's youth. The regard for work and the respect for material accumulation inherited from middle-class puritanism, and the gospel of wealth which grew out of it had, by 1900, left behind the old puritan corollary: that spending for pleasure was evil. In the 1880s spending was becoming respectable. As the new century opened, there were many who were persuaded that work no longer was. Work, for some who could afford the opinion, was now considered not only dull but unfashionable. The abundant resources of the West had made holy materialism into hedonistic materialism. On the frontier, as Vernon Parrington put it,

> Everywhere was a welling-up of primitive pagan desires after long repressions—to grow rich, to grasp power, to be strong and masterful and lay the world at its feet. It was a violent reaction from the narrow poverty of frontier life and the narrow inhibitions of backwoods religion.... It was consumed with a great hunger for abundance.... It was frankly materialistic and if material goods could be wrested from society it would lay its hands heartily to the work.

This was the mood of the late 1880s and early 1890s, into which F. Scott Fitzgerald was born. A frontier expectation of easy riches persisted into a post-frontier period when it was possible to gratify a hunger for abundance and, beyond abundance, for those things which a middle-class puritanism had linked with abundance: license in sexual matters and extravagance in spending. This was Fitzgerald's material—it did not require a Jazz Age to bring it to his attention. In 1920 he was sure that America was going on a spree and there was going to be plenty to tell about it. It was not the first spree; it was a spree which had already been interrupted twice, once by the depression of 1893 (the business setback in 1907 had not the same traumatic effect) and then by the First World War.

Fitzgerald did not say only that there was going to be plenty of fun but that there would be much work for a writer, much to report as well. Mizener's point that "his life was inextricably bound up with his work" is as true of the twenties as of any other period of his life; and work he did, though it may have been during a hangover. This golden-haired, pale, frail man with the quick smile had a nasty wit, and even his friend Edmund Wilson was always struck by "the glitter of the hard and emerald eyes." Those eyes were his way of gathering material, and his gift for a phrase provided him with a way to the $30,000 a year and

Fitzgerald's birthplace in St. Paul. From elegance he aspired to splendor.

more he earned as a writer during these years. In "Winter Dreams" he said of his fictional self: "He wanted not association with glittering things and glittering people—he wanted the glittering things themselves." That, as he recited in his *Esquire* magazine articles, required hard work, work that he resented because many glittering people did not work.

That resentment arose from being so inextricably bound up with the life he was reporting. He was no romantic; he shared and lived a set of pecuniary values even though he was aware of their fatuity. His attitude toward spending was part of what Webb called the "Easter egg psychology" of frontier regions. This psychology carried with it a distaste for sustained hard work. Mark Twain spoke of the "mirage of riches" which had drawn him westward, for Twain himself was always seeking some easy alternative to work. Another victim, according to Paul Rosenfeld, was Fitzgerald. In 1924 Rosenfeld criticized the author of *This Side of Paradise* and *The Beautiful and the Damned* on the ground that "the values of a get-rich-quick society obtain too strongly over him. A little overeager like the rest of America to arrive without having really sweated, he falls victim to the favorite delusions of the society of which he is a part, tends to indulge it in its dreams of grandeur...."

But in the next year Fitzgerald published *The Great Gatsby.* It showed that he knew the reality behind those delusions, the "foul dust floating" in their wake. These had been the dreams of the frontier, and Fitzgerald put them into words better than anyone else ever has. The frontier was

> a fresh green breast of the new world. Its vanished trees, the trees that made way for Gatsby's house, had once pandered in whispers to the last and greatest of all human dreams; for a transitory enchanted moment man must have held his breath in the presence of this continent.... [Gatsby] had come a long way to this blue lawn, and his dream must have seemed so close that he could hardly fail to grasp it. He did not know that it was already behind him, somewhere back in that vast obscurity beyond the city, where the dark fields of the republic rolled on under the night.
>
> Gatsby believed in the green light, the orgiastic future

> that year after year recedes before us. It eluded us then, but that's no matter—tomorrow we will run faster, stretch out our arms farther... and one fine morning...

This expectation of an easy inheritance was fertilized by success stories, by newspaper accounts of striking it rich, by popular preachers who told their audiences that there were "acres of diamonds" waiting for them out west. Perhaps that phrase was in Fitzgerald's mind when he composed his glittering parable of the frontier in the short story that was his favorite. "The Diamond as Big as the Ritz" tells about a family which lived in splendor cupped in a valley of solid diamond. This crystallized mirage had been discovered by a wandering ancestor who was seeking a fortune in Montana after the collapse of the Confederacy. For three generations his progeny sustained an ante-bellum life of soft, sweet-scented opulence, sacrificing often and without qualm those who stumbled upon their domain and might by revealing, destroy it.

The Washington family was committed to its own comfort at the expense of all else. They acquired the impervious, cold brilliance of the crystal they owned. Like other rich people, like tragic old Midas, they eventually turned everything and everybody into money.

Fitzgerald envied them and he pitied them. He knew them well. He was, he said, "a spoiled priest." And because of that,

> all the stories that came into my head had a touch of disaster in them—the lovely young creatures in my novels went to ruin, the diamond mountains of my short stories blew up, my millionaires were as beautiful and damned as Thomas Hardy's peasants.... I was pretty sure living wasn't the reckless, careless business people thought—this generation just younger than me.

His "vantage point," he said, "was the dividing line between two generations."

The tragedy of the fortunate, the curse of the lucky ones, is a recurring theme in Fitzgerald's work. As late as the drafting of his notes for his unfinished novel *The Last Tycoon,* he had in mind another young man, who, once having been infected by easy money, by finders-keepers, has been "completely corrupted and will spend the rest of his life looking for a chance to get something for nothing." By this time, 1940, Fitzgerald himself was equally interested in failure. He no longer was willing to pander to the dreams of sudden wealth which his readers had wanted.

It was the harsh critic of his youth, Rosenfeld, who predicted what would happen: "Should Fitzgerald finally break his mold and free himself of the compulsions of the civilization in which he grew—it might go badly with his popularity. It will be a pathetic story he will have to tell, the legend of a moon which never rose; and that is the story a certain America does not wish to hear."

Fitzgerald, in his last years, was willing to take that risk; he wrote a friend three months before his death that "all gold rushes are essentially negative" and that *The Last Tycoon* "will baffle and in some ways irritate what readers I have left." In the month of his death, he spoke of the recurrent disillusionment of "every generation since the Civil War in America [which had] the sense of being somehow about to inherit the earth." Fitzgerald could tell "the legend of the moon that never rose." His generation was the first to be conscious of the passing of the frontier mirage of wealth, the first to know that there would be no more diamond mountains, that they could wait a lifetime and never see a golden rainbow touch the earth. He had experienced that too in his youth in St. Paul. His own family history imparted a sense of shame of shabbiness, a fear of financial failure, of being led to go toward some promising horizon and then being left out there somewhere in a "bored, sprawling swollen town" on the riverbank, or, even worse, some desolate foothills hamlet even farther from civilization, "minute, dismal, and forgotten." In Montana he had seen the flotsam of the frontier living in such places "like some species developed by an early whim of nature, which on second thought had abandoned them to struggle and extermination." To him the backwash of the frontier was "the ragged edge of the universe."

It has been contended here that Fitzgerald was a regional writer of the post-frontier period. A view of his native region during the years he was growing up there shows why he was so sensitive to failure. He grew up in shabby gentility in post-frontier St. Paul, in a family which had followed the mirage and had been disappointed, in a community which had repeated that experience collectively.

The city had passed its great days in the 1880s, just before the Census Bureau officially declared the frontier to have disappeared. Then, commencing in the brutal winter of 1886–87, the agricultural hinterland experienced a devastating series of blizzards, insect invasions, droughts, and crop failures which withered the dream of a western Eden. Two-thirds of Nebraska's counties failed to produce a marketable crop for nearly seven years. More than 180,000 farmers abandoned Kansas. It was reported that 18,000 prairie schooners passed *eastward* over the Mississippi River out of Nebraska and Kansas in the early 1890s. Debts piled higher and higher; in Kansas, Nebraska, the Dakotas, and Minnesota, the average was more than one mortgage to a family. Hamlin Garland spoke an angry epitaph to the Jeffersonian dream:

> Writers and orators have lied so long about the "idyllic in farm life," and said so much about the "independent American farmer," that he himself has remained blind to the fact that [farm life has provided him with] . . . a hole to hibernate in and to sleep and eat in. . . . A dreary present and a well-nigh hopeless future.

The poet Edwin Markham said the yeoman had been "betrayed, plundered, profaned, and disinherited."

Distress on the farms drove the poor into the cities. Between 1880 and 1890 half the townships in Ohio, Indiana, Illinois, Iowa, and Michigan lost population. Then, in 1893, came a general economic collapse; 20 percent of the labor force was unemployed. In the dismal, crowded cities disinherited sons of American yeomen and disappointed immigrants suffered alike.

In these same cities, at the top, another aspect of the frontier's vitality was passing—its fluid social structure. During pioneer days, the economy of western towns had been too volatile to permit the formation of tight classes. Fitzgerald, describing St. Paul in its boom days, said it had been a "rude town . . . like

Summit Avenue in St. Paul was not named without thought—it was the avenue of capitalism's gods, a celebration of the possible. Men like James J. Hill, whose home is pictured above, had taken the concept of free enterprise and given it raw power. Fitzgerald was fascinated.

a great fish just hauled out of the Mississippi and still leaping and squirming on its bank." But in the 1890s it was settling down. The exuberant architecture of the 1880s was now considered vulgar; classicism, the architecture of propriety and class consciousness, was the vogue. Wealthy burghers returning from the Columbian Exposition aspired to its decorum and also to a place in a congealing social structure. Louis Sullivan, the rebel, said of those years that the Middle West was losing its "inventiveness, its resourcefulness, its unique daring." There was a failure of nerve. A dream had collapsed.

Fitzgerald felt, with the litmus-sensitivity he possessed, that something had gone out of the life of the region. After the frontier, as after the dreams of youth, "life was not always a progress, nor a search for new horizons, nor a going away." Sometimes, even as late as 1936, he "relaxed and pretended" like Dick Diver that it was still possible to believe in steady, uprushing progress, "that the world was all put together again by the gray-haired men of the golden nineties." (He was occasionally a little vague about his decades; in an earlier story he had gotten it right. The eighties had been golden, at least in the cities; the nineties were "the gloomy nineties.") In the somber years of his youth there was a new social system hardening above a dispirited mass and he had to negotiate that social system. That, too, was his "material"—that and what happened to its products over the next forty years.

As Mizener put it:

> This was the world Fitzgerald grew up in, desiring with all the intensity of his nature to succeed according to its standards and always conscious of hovering socially on the edge of it, alternating between assertion and uncertainty because of his acute awareness that his foothold was unsure.

This aspect of his upbringing has had ample discussion by his biographers and critics. By now everybody knows how conscious Fitzgerald was of being one of the poorest boys at a series of rich boys' schools, always short of spending money, and how he became a snob. He was too much a part of his environment not to be.

His biographers have noted how quickly his heroes were

changed to accord with the opinions of others.

Mizener had this to say:

> At every stage of his career he made a hero out of the most representative and brilliant man he knew, out of Reuben Warner, the leader of his little set in St. Paul when he was a child; out of Walker Ellis during the years in college when his dream was to make Cottage Club and the Triangle; out of Henry Strater in the last two years of college; out of Gerald Murphy on the Riviera; out of Irving Thalberg in Hollywood. "At certain moments," he wrote... "one man appropriates to himself the total significance of a time and place."

For Fitzgerald this appropriation was always by a popular figure—by a man who had general approval. He was not led to attend persons who would otherwise have been inconspicuous. To employ a term in general currency a generation later, his heroes were all "big men on campus." And none of them were poor. With the exception of Monroe Stahr, his fictional heroes, like his personal heroes, were spenders. Fitzgerald, the realist, knew what money could buy. Sex, spending, and what *Time* magazine might call romance were intertwined. The time had come when a halo surrounded expensive consumer products and the admiration of many was fixed upon the man who spent glamorously, not upon the man who made good or, indeed, *made* anything at all.

Fitzgerald's interest in wealth did, finally, at the end of his life, lead him to search out where his friends' money "came from." Long years before he had abortively thought of learning something about money as a social instrument—"to ferret out," as he then put it, "how it was garnered." In the late 1930s he began writing a book about Hollywood, which he saw as a place where "the split between the controllers of... industry and the various groups of employees is widening and leaving no place for real individualists of business... whose successes are personal achievements.... [The hero]... has held himself directly responsible to everyone with whom he has worked; he has even wanted to beat up his enemies himself. In Hollywood he is 'the last tycoon.'"

Edmund Wilson summed up Fitzgerald's notes for the setting

of the uncompleted pages of his last novel. Fitzgerald was coming around to studying the relationship of wealth to society, learning about a different kind of material. He had written from Hollywood to his daughter that he feared that she might be "accepting the standards of the cosmopolitan rich," his old subjects, the glamorous spenders, and went on to describe them in this way:

> They are homeless people, ashamed of being American, unable to master the culture of another country; ashamed, usually, of their husbands, wives, grandparents, and unable to bring up descendants of whom they could be proud, even if they had the nerve to bear them; ashamed of each other yet leaning on each other's weakness; a menace to the social order in which they live—oh, why should I go on? You know how I feel about such things.

But the great reading public, which had taken his stories for entertainment out of social prurience, had failed to detect the dark commentary which underlay everything he wrote in his last fifteen years or so. The public did not know how he felt about such things. Therefore, it is important to try to do him justice as the chronicler of a place and a time, a chronicler trapped in the "second act in American lives."

II

IF YOU WOULD KNOW A MAN, know what he admires. Giacomo Constantino Beltrami, nurtured in the Italian poetic tradition of Ariosto, was not afraid to appear ridiculous if his fixed purpose required action that the world would not esteem. Like T. E. Lawrence, who in his youth surrounded himself with life-size, pasteboard figures of the knights of old, Beltrami early selected his heroes, and throughout his life he sought to emulate their exploits even though the times were hostile to heroism.

Henry Hastings Sibley and Harvey Ellis shared Beltrami's love of the Middle Ages and his strenuous individualism. In their different ways they found that they could not dominate their circumstances, but neither permitted his circumstances to dominate him. Each insisted upon living according to a pattern of his own creation, not one of contemporary society's. Each refused to be intimidated by fashion. And each had a regard for a distant period in which colors seemed brighter, character more flamboyant, freedom broader.

Sibley was not, of course, a lone exemplar of his ideals. He was representative of a strong strain in America in his time, a strain which drew strength from Jefferson and, through Jefferson, from the French and English romantics. It was also nurtured by the German romantic movement through the influence of Emerson and Thoreau. To individualism and nostalgia, these New Englanders joined a veneration for nature and a hopefulness about the capabilities of mankind.

It has not been sufficiently emphasized by historians of the Middle West that a much later generation in this region, the generation of artists, writers, and architects just before our own, lived and thought in the spirit of this romantic tradition. The admirations of this group were for the same men Sibley had admired, and their achievements are incomprehensible unless it is recognized how much vigor they drew from their heroic insistence upon a life lived in the romantic way.

Men like Frank Lloyd Wright and Louis Sullivan admired Thoreau, who himself had spoken with approval of the artist as "so resolute a dreamer." Sullivan had set before himself the ideal of a life like Michelangelo's. However balky and peevish and intractable others might think him, however little success might come to him as the world defined success, he meant to be an artist. Wright could have been writing about himself, or Beltrami, or Harvey Ellis, when he said of Sullivan: "Like all geniuses he was an absorbed egocentric—exaggerated sensibility, boundless vitality."

Wright, reflecting upon the last two decades of the nineteenth century and the first five of the twentieth, admitted in his celebrated and successful old age: "I am a little nervous for fear that I may now be with the current. It has turned, and I am a

William Gray Purcell, who shared with Louis Sullivan a lifelong commitment to art as the center of life.

little afraid of going downstream, when all my life, I have been going upstream."

They had all begun swimming upstream during the depression years after 1893. In the artistic life of the Middle West, architecture had been the chief beneficiary of the boom of the eighties, and architecture was the chief victim of the economic collapse which spread from the farms to the cities in the early nineties. New construction flagged as promoters of large buildings told their planners to stop. It was a tragic coincidence that the "uniform ceremonious style" of the Chicago Columbian Exposition was available at precisely this time to symbolize flagging confidence and a lapse into the "classic" patterns of the past.

Economic illness weakened the resistance of the region to what Sullivan called "the virus of culture," a contagion of caution. The Midwest had had a vigorous independent culture, represented at its best in architecture, but now that culture came to be embarrassed, faltering, deferential, and false. The eighties, as Fitzgerald observed, had been "golden," bright in the colors of an autumn reaping. But after 1893 there was a transformation. The Midwest took on the dead white of winter.

Daniel Burnham's classicism spread out from Chicago, like a glacier, deadening invention, chilling exuberance throughout the region. Columned porticoes, plaster pilasters, limp-linen swags replaced brilliant organic ornament. Bleak classic façades borrowed dead forms in an effort at dignity. Architecture became lifeless and decorous in the cities. Only in the suburbs and in the small towns did the vigor of the midwestern spirit sustain itself.

In 1893 Wright, with the instincts of a salmon, began his independent practice of architecture. The tide of taste was flowing against the ideals he had learned from Sullivan, and for fifty years he did, indeed, swim upstream, in a triumphant demonstration that a man of preeminent genius may not only survive a hostile environment but help to transform it. In the suburbs and small towns at first, then, as recognition came, in larger and larger commissions, he built his practice. His career is an epic story, and like Sullivan's, it has often been told. There is no need for further adulation for these departed titans. Indeed, to emphasize again what is now a conventional appreciation for their greatness would be to join the chorus, and they disdained the opinions of the chorus. There were other men who did great things and who shared the same ideals, who have not had their measure of praise, and to whose work, as a consequence, many are still blind. Chief among them were William Gray Purcell and George Grant Elmslie.

Elmslie was a quiet man, with a compulsion for throwing things away and for avoiding the spotlight. He had met Wright when they were both very young, working for the architect Joseph Silsbee in Chicago in the late eighties. Elmslie was a Scot, born in 1871, four years younger than Wright, nine years older than Purcell. He had a dry and savage wit, and though he worked with Wright for many years, they did not like each other. When they were old, Wright would speak of "little George"; Elmslie, privately, insisted that Wright had conveniently forgotten Sullivan during the long years when the man they both considered a master was sick and poor and that Wright had only feebly rallied to his aid at the end.

Purcell was handsome, articulate, reared in comfortable circumstances in Oak Park, a suburb of Chicago, amid intelligent and considerate middle-class people. He got along with the businessmen and bankers who came to him for designs, and when architecture languished during war years, he cheerfully went off to work for the Alexander Leather Company as its advertising manager, to return to architecture when things had somewhat brightened. But he was not a "success." He had a happy way of laughing at those who were his critics during those drab years in architecture, of twitting them for their philistinism, but he had no envy. Though he never compromised his unpopular principles, he was beloved by many in his profession, even those who thought him an anachronism. (Perhaps, in a competitive world, that is one reason why they loved him.)

Purcell was brought up by his grandfather because his mother and father were estranged. His own first marriage was a disaster; then, just when his doctors told him that he was likely to die from tuberculosis, he married again. But he was generally fortunate. He and his grandfather had a remarkably open and pleasant relationship, and his second marriage lasted for forty years. He not only survived several of his doctors but worked hard and happily in a household which was bouyant to its inhabitants and its innumerable visitors. Those who shared his interests and whom he could not induce to visit him were barraged with letters. Purcell was a friend who could be a joy to be with, but he was also exhausting. He loved to talk and he loved to write. He did both very well and, despite his frail health, inexhaustibly.

After their apprenticeship with Silsbee, Elmslie and Wright moved in the late 1880s to Sullivan's office. After Wright departed in 1892, Elmslie became Sullivan's chief draftsman. In the latter part of the decade, he also became Sullivan's unadmitted partner. The firm gradually lost ground to Burnham and his followers, and, finally, in the long years of Sullivan's despondency and alcoholism, with infrequent commissions, Elmslie was his nurse and custodian. Purcell worked for the firm briefly in 1903 before commencing his own practice in Minneapolis.

Together Sullivan and Elmslie designed and saw completed a series of masterpieces: the Guaranty Building in Buffalo, the Schlesinger and Mayer store in Chicago (now Carson Pirie Scott), the Henry Babson house in Riverside, Illinois, and their highest achievement, the National Farmers' Bank of Owatonna, Minnesota. Elmslie's hand could be seen in the profuse ornament which framed the show windows of the Schlesinger store, and scholars are now busily at work trying to decide whether he or Sullivan was the dominant personality at Owatonna.

The Owatonna Bank Building marked the highest point of midwestern architectural achievement. No photograph can do it justice. It resounds with color, bright, singing color: red, blue, yellow-gold, greens. When the sunlight streams through the opalescent glass of its windows, the whole interior comes alive, responding antiphonally to the prairie sky, trees, grass, and water outside. The Owatonna bank is not a modern building; it is carefully and simply shaped, but its ornament and interior have the flaring brilliance of the nineteenth century. It blazes as Richardson's interiors blazed, as John Root's buildings blazed before the blight of classicism came to bleach color away.

After the Owatonna bank was completed in 1908, there was a period in which there was little work for Sullivan and Elmslie. Elmslie finally left in despair and went to Minneapolis to join Purcell. Sullivan pulled himself together to design three more great bank buildings, smaller than Owatonna but each a wonder

Elslie and Purcell attacked the problem of the fifty-foot lot as a poet might attack the restrictions of the sonnet form (above, the E.S. Hoyt house, Red Wing, Minnesota).

to startle the eye amid the muddle of Main Street: Grinnell, Iowa (1914); Sidney, Ohio (1918); and Columbus, Wisconsin (1919). There were others, in Algona and Cedar Rapids, Iowa; Newark, Ohio; and West Lafayette, Indiana; but they were created either in times of flagging capacity or on budgets so bare that there was little Sullivan could do.

Though Purcell had worked in Sullivan's office only briefly, he was a convert to Sullivan's architectural theories. Far more articulate than Elmslie, he possessed a solid sense of design, a capacity for technical innovation, a generous spirit which drew the best out of his colleagues, and, through his grain-broker father, a large acquaintanceship with midwesterners of some means who were potential clients for the firm. He and Elmslie focused upon domestic architecture (a field in which Sullivan had little interest) and continued to respond to the desire of small-town bankers to seek novel and beautiful solutions to their building problems.

Their largest completed commissions were banks for Winona and Madison, Minnesota, and Rhinelander, Wisconsin. Their smaller banks were more successful than Sullivan's; his efforts at Algona and Newark lack the power of their little buildings in Adams, Leroy, or Grand Meadow, Minnesota. Purcell and Elmslie rescued William L. Steele, a colleague from their Chicago days, when he was given a large commission beyond his capabilities, and together they created one of America's most arresting buildings in the "skyscraper" Woodbury County Courthouse for Sioux City, Iowa. It is truly baroque, festooned with monumental ornament, its lobby overwhelming in richness.

Purcell and Elmslie had only a decade to work together. The First World War, like the depression of 1893, brought construction to a halt. The followers of Sullivan were, for their various reasons, unable to survive the war as a concerted school of practitioners who shared the same ideals and the same determination to resist the prevailing classicism. Frank Lloyd Wright was an expatriate in Japan, beset by domestic tragedy. Walter Burley Griffin had departed for Australia. Sullivan himself was sick, his life drawing to a despairing end. Purcell, always prone to tuberculosis, was told by his doctors that he had only a short time to live and that he must abandon the vigorous practice of architecture. He went to the West Coast, and though he designed many good houses in his remaining years, most of his energies were devoted to supporting, through a stream of articles and letters, the ideals of Sullivan. Elmslie returned to Chicago and sustained a desultory practice until his death in 1952. Others of the original group relapsed into popular classicism, or half-timberesque suburban, or Spanish colonial or whatever sold at the moment.

As early as 1940 Purcell was written off as a crotchety old fellow by some critics. But in 1965 he was still resolute, still handsome. Though his body was very, very tired, there was nothing tired about his extraordinary eyes. Out of the wreath of wrinkles they still shone, illuminated by his will and his wit. For all these years that will had kept him alive. He had steadfastly refused to accommodate the predictions of the medical profession and was still ready to do battle for his principles and Sullivan's.

He was eighty-five, the last survivor of Sullivan's staff. Despite the greater fame which Frank Lloyd Wright had so purposefully earned, Purcell was Sullivan's true prophet. Wright had moved beyond Sullivan; in iron egotism he had broken through the hostility of most of his profession and the indifference of most of the public. He was contemptuous of nearly all his contemporaries, even those who might subscribe to the same principles. His associates were but pencils in his masterful hand; he could have no colleague.

Purcell, on the other hand, was always ready to exhort, encourage, and praise. Though his chief effort was to gain for Sullivan the admiration he deserved, Purcell also brought to the attention of readers of architectural periodicals the unheeded work of other men of an older generation, such as Bernard Maybeck and Harvey Ellis, and wrote a series of studies on his own contemporaries.

From 1909 to 1917, Purcell and Elmslie had built residences for clients in Iowa, Wisconsin, North Dakota, California, Massachusetts, Illinois, and Minnesota. In small towns in the Midwest they delight the traveler with their unexpected gaiety; there is vigor in their wooden and terra-cotta ornament, and a profusion of subtle grace in the stained glass and mosaic work which Elmslie lavished on the smallest commissions. Purcell said of him that "he just poured it out—Chopin with a pencil." The importance of their domestic work is now beginning to receive its due.

But it is the banks of Purcell and Elmslie, of Sullivan and Elmslie, and of Sullivan alone which show best the relationship of progressive architecture to the main themes of this book. These were the final and probably the finest expression of the romantic spirit in the Midwest. Those who thought Fitzgerald was romantic (when he was merely snobbish) failed to see what could be romantic about designing a bank for Algona, Iowa, or Hector, Minnesota. Of course the answer lies in the way the designer felt about the job.

The romantic tradition, with its veneration for the Middle Ages, emphasized the dignity of handcrafts, of things for use. Viollet le Duc, John Ruskin, and William Morris idealized the ethos of the cathedral builders, and their belief in such a medieval ethos actually created a modern one. From England Morris's ideas spread to America, where the arts and crafts movement was very strong in the 1880s. Harvey Ellis found some solace in his later years working for Gustav Stickley's Morrisite workshops, and George Elmslie came from a family of Scottish Morrisites. Purcell asserted a point of view which united William Morris, Frank Lloyd Wright, Louis Sullivan, and himself:

"The free organic architects realized the all-inclusive character of the building arts . . . and pressed to develop all possible links . . . [to] provide painters with walls, glass makers with windows, needle workers with fabrics to stitch in colors, sculptors with stones. . . ." This was no self-conscious artiness, no invidious display of the fine arts for a cultivated few. It was instead a statement that art and life are the same thing, that commerce and art should not be mutually exclusive. Even the cockpit of commerce, the bank, could be ennobled. Magnificence need not be reserved for princes but should be familiar to all citizens, not just on ceremonial occasions but daily in the marketplace. This is an insufficiently honored part of the romantic tradition: things in regular use were respected, from kitchen utensils, bowls, and towels, to skyscraper buildings and prairie banks. The groups around William Morris in England and around Louis Sullivan in Chicago did not disdain the design of such things. Sullivan, Purcell, Elmslie, and Wright did not feel "reduced" to commercial architecture. They welcomed such commissions, and there was nothing perfunctory in the way they executed them. They, like Horatio Greenough, felt that their attitudes toward their work would "do for all structure from a bedstead to a cathedral."

Here was the intersection of frontier materialism and the romantic tradition. Frontiersmen often made beautiful what might have been merely useful: a canoe or an axe handle was given what Walt Whitman would call "a comely shape," rosemaling ornamented kitchen cupboards; it was amazing how quickly a bed of flowers came to bloom by the door of a sod house.

It has been contended by so eminent a critic as Van Wyck Brooks that the midwestern frontier was a bare and squalid place, impatient of art, narrowly concerned with grubbing out riches. This reading of history led Henry Adams and Brooks to think that the Midwest was redeemed from barbarism by the classicist influences, which began to dominate in 1893. There has been a strange alliance between these exponents of a seaboard provincialism and the Marxist critics of a later day, who, recognizing the bourgeois spirit of the Middle West, were certain that it could not have produced great art. Francis Swales, as has been noted, regretted what he thought the West had done to Harvey Ellis; and even as late as 1960 some critics were still misreading the record and thereby missing what, with deference to Brooks, might be called the flowering of the Old Northwest.

This flowering had been most profuse in the 1880s, when commerce and the arts moved unselfconsciously together. A second component of the romantic tradition, splendid individualism, was then manifested in the freebooting tycoons who sponsored the best work of the greatest architects: John J. Glessner, the farm machinery manufacturer, and Marshall Field commissioned Richardson's buildings. Charles R. Crane, Harley Bradley, Avery Coonley, and the redoubtable Ferdinand Peck (of the Auditorium Building) made possible the achievements of Sullivan, Wright, and their colleagues.

"Business is a dull game," said Fitzgerald in the 1930s. But it was neither dull nor blind to art in the 1880s. These colorful entrepreneurs welcomed innovation in architecture as they did in business and deferred to no desiccated arbiter of taste to tell them what was a good building.

Purcell and Wright insisted that they represented a continuous tradition of an interplay between "free, democratic, and truly 'organic'" risk-taking businessmen and the arts.

Purcell said: "Sullivan was actually keeping alive the vigorous American tradition of the 1870s and 1880s.... Sullivan was a true traditionalist carrying on the living fire that bozart [Purcell's epithet for Burnhamism] was destroying.... [The classicists were] proud and gorgeous courtiers ... who dwelt in imported art forms caught up in a conventional etiquette...."

And there is plenty of evidence to support the hypothesis that risk-taking, innovation, and unrepentant commercial individualism are sympathetic circumstances for the arts, once bare subsistence has been achieved.

Such a proposition is suggested by a comment of John Maynard Keynes, offered "as a thesis for those who like rash generalizations ... by far the larger portion of the world's great writers and artists have flourished in an atmosphere of buoyancy, exhilaration and the freedom from economic cares which is engendered by profit inflations." As an Englishman he thought particularly of the boom times when buccaneers like Francis Drake and John Hawkins enriched good Queen Bess by hijacking the Spanish galleons bearing the riches of the first American frontier. "Never in the annals of the modern world has there existed so prolonged and so rich an opportunity for the business man, the speculator, and the profiteer. In these golden years modern capitalism was born."

Wayne Andrews has related Keynes's intuition to the United States, suggesting that

> the most vital American architecture of any given time will usually be located in those communities where the most new money was being made and enjoyed. The Boston of Charles Bulfinch or the Salem of Samuel McIntire were swarming with aggressive businessmen at the moment the buildings we cherish were going up. As for the Virginia of "Westover" and "Stratford," it was neither wistful nor serene, but one of the most enterprising colonies in which alert real estate speculators, usually men of no antecedents, were bidding with undisguised eagerness for bigger and bigger land grants. Chicago of the 1880s and '90s, surely

Purcell operated, like Sullivan, on the conviction that art must be put in the service of the people, and as an architect-artist he maintained that art was less invention than a distillation: "The architect of a successful building is really not a designer, an originator—but an organizer, a discoverer, one who tries to find something that already exists." Above is the home he "discovered" for himself in Lake Place, Minneapolis, in 1913.

one of the crudest of cities, is justly celebrated as the birth-place of much of what we call modern architecture.

It was in the spirit of the 1880s that the banks of Sullivan, Purcell and Elmslie were being created between 1907 and 1924. Their sponsors were bankers who still sustained the free, risk-taking spirit of that time, who still were important factors in detonating change in the economy.

Seeing these bank buildings as they are (not merely as they appear in photographs, shrunken and drained of color) makes this clear. They are not ornamented safes. They are not tombs for money. They are places where money is in motion, places for the transaction of trade, where men come and go for business. Fitzgerald missed this aspect of the matter. Sullivan did not regard this kind of business as a dull game.

The romantic architects did not feel themselves estranged from independent and daring businessmen; they shared a common respect for strenuous personality. Vehement individualism has always been a part of the romantic tradition, and the individualism of a James J. Hill was not so different from that of Napoleon Bonaparte or, for that matter, of Frank Lloyd Wright. Wright asserted that "the mind of the superior businessman was more free than the pseudocultural academic to accept the change that is progress." Purcell made it clear that Wright was not talking about the corporate bureaucrat: "the free, democratic, and truly 'organic' business mind of that day was certainly far, far different from the . . . power-conscious economic royalists [and] . . . the manipulators of trusts."

The respect that Wright, Sullivan, and Purcell expressed for the strong individualists among businessmen was reciprocated. Here is an explanation of the fact that after Sullivan fell from favor in the cities, he still received commissions from small-town bankers in Ohio, Wisconsin, Iowa, and Minnesota. After Chicago had passed into the hands of the classicists, Sullivan was kept alive by commissions provided by bankers like J. R. Wheeler of Columbus, Wisconsin, and Carl K. Bennett of Owatonna, Minnesota.

In the period between the recovery from the 1893 depression and the decline of the farm economy in the middle 1920s (which carried downward with it the vitality of small market towns), small-town bankers were still among the "last tycoons." They were among the successful of the first frontier generation, and they still held power in their communities. Not yet completely at the mercy of national economic forces, they had the self-confidence of men who could diagnose the common diseases of local economic life and who had a shelf of remedies for those which were curable. "I thought of it as being just sound banking," said Wheeler; "we encouraged experimental farming techniques, got the farmers to work closely with the County Agent, promoted the canning industry in order to guarantee the farmers a market, and did other things of the sort. But I had never really thought about these things in quite the same way before I met Sullivan as I did afterwards."

Sullivan could make businessmen see themselves in a new way. He inspired them, but he required a receptive environment. The soil had to be ready, and it was, in the small towns. Carl Bennett was ready in Owatonna:

> It was determined to make a search for an architect whose aim it was to express the thought or use underlying a building, adequately, without fear of precedent—like a virtuoso shaping his material into new forms of use and beauty. From this search finally emerged the name of one who, though possibly not fully understood or appreciated at first, seemed to handle the earth-old materials in virile and astonishingly beautiful forms of expression. The owners of this building feel that they have a true and lasting work of art—a structure which, though built for business, will be as fresh and inspiring in its beauty one hundred years from now as it is today.

The search of which Bennett spoke was an extension of the restless innovating of the frontier. In those days towns like Owatonna were led by men who assumed that the answers to most questions had not yet been found, and they were not yet so terrorized by the nationalization of commerce (or of taste) as to think themselves unworthy of helping to find some of those answers. They were, perhaps, arrogant. But they were willing to take risks.

These small-town bankers had their glory. They had helped

to organize struggling camps of prairie colonists and to make cities out of them. It was the confidence they gained from that experience which made them fit to be the patrons of great architecture. Said Purcell:

> Many critics said that the Owatonna bank was no bank for a farming community. Sullivan said that the farming community of Owatonna was the very sort of community that would know exactly what he was talking about. And they did. They all loved the building... [but] it was the aristocrats of literature, of criticism, of architecture, of art of the time, and particularly of business and banking where it had become monopolistic that were against this architecture, and their claim that the people would not accept it and not understand it was due to the fact that they were afraid of it. They couldn't just tell why, but they just couldn't tolerate too much democracy around. The voice of the people for them had to be the voice of the right people, and the right people were those who had the voice and thought that corresponded exactly to what they wanted to accomplish.

Here was another romantic theme in the creed of the progressive architects: their belief in the high capacity of men of all classes and conditions. This was the creed that had animated Sibley's era of reform, and it was still strong in the Progressive politics of the early twentieth century. Purcell put it in these words: "We believed that a humane and democratic approach to all one's fellow human beings means cooperation from us in their desire to see, to find out, and to participate." Sullivan had said that the mission of architecture was "lifting the eyelids of the world."

The committed artist was Purcell's ideal, the artist involved in a constant dialogue with his neighbors in the midst of daily life. The commitment of the artist would, of course, be fruitless and his willingness to engage in a dialogue remain unconsummated unless there were a public capable of responding.

Purcell, Sullivan, and Wright were inheritors of the transcendentalist strain of Jeffersonian philosophy. Wright inherited it from his Unitarian-Universalist preacher-father, one of whose early pastorates was in the midst of transcendentalism's native heath, suburban Boston. For Purcell the link was through his grandfather, William Cunningham Gray.

Gray was a journalist who had been born in an Ohio log cabin in 1830 and then went west to share the frontier experience. In Oak Park, Illinois, he became a newspaper proprietor and the first nationally syndicated columnist, reporting on the triumphs of westering (such as the laying of the golden spike) and the failures of industrialism. Purcell proudly said of his grandfather that he "first brought to public attention the deplorable conditions of child labor in the cotton mills." Gray sustained the reforming spirit of his youth through the degrading years after the Civil War. He was a Progressive Republican and then a Bull-mooser, a leader of the intellectual life of Oak Park during the years when it provided a haven to Frank Lloyd Wright and support for John Peter Altgeld, Robert La Follette, and Theodore Roosevelt.

Gray's devotion to the cause of reform was nourished by roots in the reforming enthusiasm of his generation. He provided a link between that generation and the Progressive movement. In his own writings could be heard the echo of Jefferson, who wrote in 1826 that "all eyes are opened, or opening, to the rights of man," and of Emerson who rejoiced in 1844: "What a fertility of projects for the salvation of the world!" That fertility, with its ripening crop of reform, was blasted by the Civil War and lay fallow for forty years. But men like Gray were there to remember and to plant a new crop.

One of the reasons why Purcell is so interesting is that while he lived until 1965, he never lost touch with the transcendentalist reformers. Because he had been brought up by his grandfather, he had been "well-conditioned with the Lincoln era and the pioneer men of the middle border ... because of the skipped generation—the skipped intellectual world.... I actually experienced the '60s and '70s because ... all the things that I touched every day ... came into our family when my grandparents had been married December 2, 1856."

In Sullivan, Purcell found another son of transcendentalism. Like many other young men of the Progressive period who had read Emerson and Thoreau and who were persuaded by their eloquence, Purcell found in Sullivan's rhetoric something both familiar and heady in its fresh application to his own time. This was a mystical attitude toward nature, a component of faith in natural man. Thoreau had gone forth into nature for a season and had returned in the old Yankee way to preach to those who had remained behind, and Sullivan, too, regarded nature as a fruitful source of sermons.

To Sullivan nature meant not merely trees and water and wind, the scent of pine and the song of the warbler, but the place in which man could find himself without distraction. He hated cities as Wright hated them, because they shut man off from nature. He hated bad architecture for the same reason. Instead of exalting man, enobling his daily tasks, bad architecture was apart from him, intimidating him, chilling him, constricting him in the mold of convention and drudgery.

Purcell understood Sullivan's passion, and he knew from whence it came. Writing to a friend about Van Wyck Brooks's *The Flowering of New England,* he pointed out that "Sullivan himself, as a schoolboy, sat under Moses Woolson, who was the immediate product of the flowering of New England. . . . [The] most potent fruit of the first half of the nineteenth century was Louis Sullivan."

Here, at the core of Progressive belief, Sullivan, Gray, and Thoreau stood together. They were all saying the same thing. Nature was a place for conscious confrontation with reality, a liturgy of transcendental belief. Every summer Gray would take Purcell to live on an island in northern Wisconsin thirty miles from any town or neighbor except for his Indian friends. That island was kept very primitive physically but, in the tradition of Thoreau, very sophisticated intellectually. In this western Walden there was little furniture but plenty of ideas. In conversation the intellect was honed on the concepts of the German idealists, the French physiocrats, the Hindu epic poets, and the New England transcendentalists. Nature was to be felt through senses made acute by a focused intention to feel and to understand. The dialogue with nature was the same as the dialogue with art: it required a fresh and willing intelligence, a dedication tempered by conviction.

It was inevitable that Thoreau's image should have fused in Purcell's mind with Grandfather Gray's. Characteristically, he remembered exactly when that event occurred. It was at 11:45 on the night of December 31, 1899:

> I got home from some party . . . and quite excited about the beginning of the new century, stood in the wide upper hall before Grandfather Gray's portrait, waiting for the New Year's bells to ring.
>
> On the opposite wall under the lamp [were] . . . the bookshelves which he had had in his college room in 1848–50. My eye fell upon the green volumes of Thoreau. I took one out and stood there reading for ten minutes. Outside the snow creaked and whined under an occasional passing iron wheel—and the light on the street corner glinted through the prisms of the leaded windows of the door to the porch. This was my introduction to Thoreau. . . . I was nineteen years old and Grandfather Gray was seventy. As I turned out the light and went to my room I thought of my future—wondered what it would be for me—but never doubting that it would be very wonderful. And it has been.

His introduction to Sullivan had occurred earlier, and one of the reasons why his life was indeed very wonderful was that Sullivan provided him with an immutable faith in his role as an architect and in his Progressive creed. Neither illness nor the unpopularity of his ideas diminished his fervor for the principles of Sullivan and of his grandfather. He was kindly, generous with praise for others' work, never insistent upon recognition for himself, but very, very tough. He never relinquished the commitment he made in 1889, and through him can be perceived how strong the transcendentalist creed could be.

> In Chicago one cold January night—the 25th it was—when I was nine, a clattering brougham took us on its iron tires through the dark, cobbled granite streets, to climb at last those velvet stairs—look up into the magic world of Sullivan's great . . . 4,200 seat Assembly Hall of the American people. Way, way up there, twinkled the just-accomplished miracle of electric lights—lights by the millions to me—there in that firmament of beautiful golden arcs. In that moment I became an architect.

From that moment he shared Sullivan's commitment to art as the center of life.

Despite the long decades of disappointment which followed

Sullivan's relatively brief success, the master never regarded himself as apart from the life of his nation. He wept for the degradation of its taste and suffered hunger rather than give it what it wanted, but he never pulled himself away from it. He was always hopeful that it would return to its best self, and, in time it did – at least it came to know what it had lost in not drawing upon his power during those years.

Purcell had the same confidence – and the same commitment. He had found his paradigm in his tenth year, and though he knew well Sullivan's frailties, alcoholism, despondency, and crankiness, he also knew that Sullivan was a great man. His discipleship never flagged. Once he had taken up Sullivan's cause, he was undeterred by the fact that his hero was, in the eyes of most of the world, a failure.

Here is an extraordinary achievement: Purcell could write of Sullivan that "to once become a part of his adventure puts you into a new firmament of freedom, opportunity; the trail to be followed is up, out, and it is limitless." He saw before him a sick and drunken man doing small commissions for back-country banks, designing drinking fountains and lightpoles, and in his understanding that broken figure acquired grandeur. It was what Sullivan meant to be, not what he was, which was important. It is hard for any man wholly to admire a contemporary; the temptation to envy or disdain is very strong. But it was within Purcell's generous spirit to admire a contemporary as graceless and unpopular as Sullivan, and to share his ideals.

It is sometimes useful to recall the degree to which the writers of the 1850s who were read by Sullivan and Purcell imported into the American scene the brilliant colors of the Middle Ages, how their reading of chronicles and romances heightened their exaltation of the individuality of American figures. Francis Parkman, one of Purcell's favorites, could look upon Sieur de La Salle up to his waist in Mississippi ooze, surrounded by a swarm of mosquitoes, and write about him thus:

> Beset by a throng of enemies, he stands, like the King of Israel, head and shoulders above them all. He was a tower of adamant against whose impregnable front hardship and danger, the rage of man and of the elements, the southern sun, the northern blast, fatigue, famine, disease, delay, dis-

> appointment, and deferred hope emptied their quivers in vain. That very pride which, Coriolanus-like, declared itself most sternly in the thickest press of foes, has in it something to challenge admiration. Never, under the impenetrable mail of paladin or crusader, beat a heart of more intrepid mettle than within the stoic panoply that armed the breast of La Salle.

When a mind is full of images such as these, it can sustain itself with considerable mettle against public indifference. Sullivan's identification with Michelangelo as "a superman... a great Free Spirit... mighty man of courage" is understandable, just as is Purcell's indifference to what the critics said of Sullivan. Wright's famous arrogance was strengthened by a heroic purpose. But it is crucial to the understanding of their art that it be stressed that they were romantic artists in a uniquely American way. Their reverence for nature required them to apply their talents to the creation of suburban homes for the many and to the ennobling of buildings meant for commerce. This is romanticism with a severely practical effect. A European architect asked Purcell about "peasant culture," and he replied:

> If you know the peasant as he truly is when not suffering under the effects of long misrule, then you will see that the free and natural man expresses himself with an intelligence, wisdom – poetry and completeness which city-conditioning and gadget-worship [have] largely destroyed. This Natural Man in his full powers is, of course, the only Aristocrat.

This was why Purcell, Elmslie, and Sullivan were not surprised when they found clients who understood the Progressive creed. And it was also why they were proud to lavish their genius upon small-town buildings, why they made glittering things for people others may have thought dull.

"Great poets need great audiences," said Whitman.

"If you would seek and express the best that is in yourself," Louis Sullivan said to a young architect, "you must search out the best that is in your people.... in their hearts they seek honest and fearless men, men simple and clear of mind, loyal to their own manhood and to the people."

Bibliographic Notes

Giacomo Constantino Beltrami / Stephen Harriman Long

Beltrami's *A Pilgrimage to America* was reprinted in 1962, and a sketch of his life by A. J. Hill was reprinted in 1889 (Vol. II, Minn. Hist. Coll. 183). There is a new biography of Long by Richard G. Wood, *Stephen Harriman Long, 1784-1864* (1966), which in tone and style matches the subject. The standard work on his western travels is Edwin James's, in Reuben Thwaite's edition of *Early Western Travels, 1748-1846* (1904–6). William H. Keating's *Narrative* of Long's Minnesota adventures was reprinted in 1959. Obviously, I found Chrétien de Troyes and Walter Map helpful in understanding Beltrami's medievalism. The reader who is intrigued by the court of Eleanor of Aquitaine will find a vast literature before him. My personal favorites in this general area are Huizinga's *The Waning of the Middle Ages* (1954), Amy Kelly's *Eleanor and the Four Kings* (1958), Charles H. Haskins's *The Renaissance of the 12th Century* (1957), and Jessie L. Weston's *From Ritual to Romance* (1957), but I am sure that each of these has its supporters and detractors among specialists. It might be equally interesting to look for Beltrami's progenitors in Novalis or in the Italian epicists of the early Renaissance, Boiardo and Ariosto.

Henry Hastings Sibley / Alexander Ramsey

The official biographer of Sibley, Nathaniel West (*The Ancestry, Life, and Times of the Hon. Henry Hastings Sibley* (1889), is unjust to the old gentleman he knew by presuming that he was born an old gentleman. Sibley's own writings can be found in his unfinished autobiography, published in Minneapolis in 1932; in contemporary periodical literature, particularly *The Spirit of the Times*; and in his biography of "Iron Face" Frazier, reprinted in 1950. Wilson P. Shortridge's study of Sibley, *The Transition of a Typical Frontier,* was published in 1922. *Minnesota History* published the latest of a number of short studies of aspects of his career in its Spring, 1969, issue. Books examining the American Adam on the frontier have been frequent of late. The best are Henry Nash Smith's *Virgin Land* (1950), Roy Harvey Pierce's *Savagism and Civilization* (1953), Lewis O. Saum's *The Fur Trader and the Indian* (1965), Leo Marx's *The Machine in the Garden* (1964), R. W. B. Lewis's *The American Adam* (1955), and for an entrancing high-church version, David Noble's *The Eternal Adam and the New World Garden* (1968).

Bare (or, rather, overclothed) glimpses of Sibley and Ramsey as they really were can be found in the establishment histories of Minnesota, that of William W. Folwell and that of Returne I. Holcombe and his colleagues, each in four volumes. For scholars there are manuscript materials in the Minnesota Historical Society which tell more of the story, though most of the comtemporaries were very careful in their remarks.

The only critical work on Ramsey, generally the object of the most abject filiopietistic writings in Minnesota, is John C. Haugland's excellent but unpublished thesis, "Alexander Ramsey and the Republican Party, 1855-1875," available from the University of Minnesota Library (1961). W. H. C. Folsom's *Fifty Years in the Old Northwest* (1888), adulates with a wink, and Major T. M. Newson's *Pen Pictures* (1886) snaps at the great man's heals without biting. Ramsey awaits a definitive biography.

Harvey Ellis / Daniel Burnham

There is no biography of Harvey Ellis. I have done sketches of his life in *Minnesota History* (Fall, 1966), in *The American West* (March, 1968), and, at greater length, in *The Prairie School Review* (1st Quarter, 1968), which also carries two good older sketches, one by Hugh M. G. Garden and one by Claude Bragdon, which is much like that appearing in Bragdon's *Merely Players* (1929). All the known references in periodical literature to Ellis and his work appear in the bibliographical note in *The Prairie School Review* and in Eileen Manning Michel's unpublished master's thesis (1953), which may be obtained from the library of the University of Minnesota.

The accredited biography of Daniel Burnham is the unctuous product of Charles Moore, an associate and a dedicated disciple of Burnham's last, colonial-classicist phase: *Daniel Hudson Burnham-Architect, Planner of Cities* (1921). There is a welcome rumor afloat that a new and critical biography is in process at the University of Wisconsin. Harriet Monroe's biography *John Wellborn Root* (1896) was reprinted in 1966 by the Prairie School Press, Chicago, and in the following year the Horizon Press reprinted, with splendid illustrations, Donald Hoffman's collection of a number of Root's articles under the title *The Meanings of Architecture.*

The derogatory opinions upon Burnham of the Wright-Sullivan-Purcell group can be found scattered through their writings, but a fair sampling appears in Sullivan's *The Autobiography of an Idea* (1924), as reprinted in a 1966 Dutton paperback, *The Literature of Architecture.* A Meridian paperback of *Frank Lloyd Wright's Writings and Buildings,* masterfully edited by Edgar Kaufmann and Ben Raeburn (1960), carries Wright's splenetic comments in its early pages. The defense of Burnham, or at least a less armageddonous view of his contest with Sullivan, can be found in Christopher Tunnard and Henry Hope Reed's *The American Skyline* (1956) and in John Burchard and Albert Bush-Brown's *The Architecture of America* (1966).

Ignatius Donnelly / Frank Billings Kellogg

All the necessary biographical material concerning Ignatius Donnelly has been culled out by Martin Ridge for his *Ignatius Donnelly* (1962), an excellent, dispassionate, painstaking book. Everybody else who writes about midwestern politics has only a chapter or snippet on Donnelly. Russell M. Nye's otherwise excellent *Midwestern Progressive Politics* (1951) is marred by some factual errors about Donnelly. Eric Goldman's *Rendezvous with Destiny* (1951) is a little too breezy and a little too patronizing about the agrarian rebels, and also stumbles on a fact or two. Larzer Ziff's *The American 1890's* (1966) takes the opposite point of view to that expressed by this author, perhaps because Ziff is concerned more with literature than with politics, perhaps because he is offended by the mores of the Bible Belt. Richard Hofstadter's *American Political Tradition* (1948) is a splendid job of rethinking about a number of major figures in that tradition, which unfortunately did not extend to rethinking about Donnelly.

There are a number of good economic or general histories of the period, of which I found four especially useful: Harold U. Faulkner's *Politics, Reform and Expansion* (1959); Cochrane and Miller's *The Age of Enterprise* (1961); David Potter's *People of Plenty* (1954), a study of national character in historical terms; and Matthew Josephson's classic *The Robber Barons* (1962 ed.).

Milton Friedman's big book is (with Anna J. Schwartz) *A Monetary History of the United States* (1963). There are good chapters on economics in particular in John B. Hicks's great *The Populist Revolt* (1931). The census reports are, of course, the primary documents for statistics, though other sources are mentioned in the text.

The Donnelly papers are largely (and large they are) in the Minnesota Historical Society, although some family members in St. Paul still retain interesting pieces.

Frank B. Kellogg has had a biographer, David Bryn-Jones, who did not chew very hard on his material *Frank B. Kellogg: A Biography* (1937). A much better treatment of the effect of his attitudes upon foreign policy is an unpublished Ph.D. thesis by Richard Cleaver (1956). In understanding blue and red Progressivism, I found most useful the following: Otis L. Graham, Jr.'s *An Encore for Reform* (1967) and Russell M. Nye's *Midwestern Progressive Politics* (1951), though, of course, there is much else on the subject—the literature on Theodore Roosevelt, Woodrow Wilson, and their times is inexhaustible.

Kellogg was, for one so celebrated, the recipient of very little scholarly attention. A spate of books discussed the Kellogg-Briand pact, but those interested in the man will have to turn to the voluminous Kellogg papers at the Minnesota Historical Society. Mr. and Mrs. Kent Kreider of Hamline University have turned to them with a will and with a capacity for imaginative reconstruction and illuminating analogy which promises a great historical essay when their labors are done.

F. Scott Fitzgerald / William Gray Purcell

The card catalogues of the libraries are filling with biographies and critical studies of Fitzgerald, and around St. Paul there are still a score of people who can retail unpublished tales about him. But, of course, Fitzgerald was a writer, and his own work tells more about him than do all the words spun by others.

Purcell, on the other hand, published only one book, *The St. Croix Trail* (1965), and that posthumously. It is the reminiscence of a frail old man, edited without much understanding. There is nothing in print that gives any sense of his warmth and his merciless honesty except a few of his lead articles in the *Northwest Architect*, which are now hard to find, and his incredibly profuse correspondence, which reposes in the great archive we have assembled for the University of Minnesota and which we hope will shortly be properly disposed for the pleasure of scholars and friends of a lively architecture. David Gebhard's definitive work on Purcell and Elmslie still awaits a responsive publisher, though it can be found in the early form of his Ph.D. thesis in the University of Minnesota Library.

To the reader who wishes to know more about the Prairie School group, I can recommend the following: Vincent Scully's short essay on Frank Lloyd Wright in the Braziller *Masters of Modern Architecture* (1960) series has infuriated some of the pedants, but it is eloquent, detonative writing. Albert Bush-Brown's parallel sketch of Louis Sullivan in the same series is also good. Willard Connely's *Louis Sullivan, As He Lived* (1960) is an excellent reconstruction by a man who can empathize; Hugh Morrison's critical study, *Louis Sullivan: Prophet of Modern Architecture* (1935), is still the accredited work on the buildings. John Szarkowski's *Idea of Louis Sullivan* (1956) has magnificent illustrations and miraculously catches the "idea." There are two big surveys of the Chicago school and its setting, social and technical: Carl Condit's *The Chicago School of Architecture* (1964), which emphasizes engineering, and Hugh D. Duncan's *Culture and Democracy* (1965), which presents the social and intellectual background in Chicago.

The standard histories of American architecture slight Purcell and Elmslie, yet there is such a glut of books on Wright that all one can do is wave the reader toward the stacks with a recommendation to lay in provisions for a month. Wright is his own best, though perhaps not most accurate, biographer, and Sullivan's works are now being reissued in paperback. One can apprehend Wright-as-public-figure from Wright. But there really is no book, as yet, which helps us put all these men into the broad midwestern scene from which they came.

Picture Credits

All illustrations for *Men on the Moving Frontier* were obtained through the courtesy of the Minnesota Historical Society with the exception of the following: Pages 6, 7: Roger Olmsted. Page 13: Nebraska State Historical Society. Pages 20, 32: Bancroft Library, University of California. Page 36: Public Archives of Canada. Pages 58, 61: National Anthropological Archives, Smithsonian Institution. Page 92: Chicago Historical Society. Page 93: Tom Knudtsen. Pages 96, 97: Roger Olmsted. Page 101: Hedrich-Blessing Photographs.

Index

The text for this book is Garamond No. 3, with Palatino chapter heads, both set in Linofilm by Applied Typographic Systems, Palo Alto, California. The book was printed and bound by the George Banta Company, Menasha, Wisconsin. The paper is Hilding Hi-Bulk, cream white, and the cloth is from Holliston Mills, Northwood, Massachusetts.

Design by John Beyer.